TRIALS AND
CONFESSIONS
OF
A HOUSEKEEPER

T. S. ARTHUR

1st WORLD
LIBRARY
Literary Society

Trials and Confessions of a Housekeeper

T. S. Arthur

© 1st World Library, 2006
PO Box 2211
Fairfield, IA 52556
www.1stworldlibrary.com
First Edition

LCCN: 2006907737

Softcover ISBN: 1-4218-2454-X
Hardcover ISBN: 1-4218-2354-3
eBook ISBN: 1-4218-2554-6

Purchase *"Trials and Confessions of a Housekeeper"*
as a traditional bound book at:
www.1stWorldLibrary.com/purchase.asp?ISBN=1-4218-2454-X

1st World Library is a literary, educational organization
dedicated to:

- Creating a free internet library of downloadable ebooks

- Hosting writing competitions and offering book
  publishing scholarships.

Interested in more 1st World Library books?
contact: literacy@1stworldlibrary.com
Check us out at: www.1stworldlibrary.com

1st World Library Literary Society

Giving Back to the World

"If you want to work on the core problem, it's early school literacy."

- James Barksdale, former CEO of Netscape

"No skill is more crucial to the future of a child, or to a democratic and prosperous society, than literacy."

- Los Angeles Times

Literacy... means far more than learning how to read and write... The aim is to transmit... knowledge and promote social participation."

- UNESCO

"Literacy is not a luxury, it is a right and a responsibility. If our world is to meet the challenges of the twenty-first century we must harness the energy and creativity of all our citizens."

- President Bill Clinton

"Parents should be encouraged to read to their children, and teachers should be equipped with all available techniques for teaching literacy, so the varying needs and capacities of individual kids can be taken into account."

- Hugh Mackay

INTRODUCTION

UNDER the title of Confessions of a Housekeeper, a portion of the matter in this volume has already appeared. The book is now considerably increased, and the range of subjects made to embrace the grave and instructive, as well as the agreeable and amusing. The author is sure, that no lady reader, familiar with the trials, perplexities, and incidents of housekeeping, can fail to recognize many of her own experiences, for nearly every picture that is here presented, has been drawn from life.

CONTENTS

CHAPTER I

MY SPECULATION IN CHINA WARE

THIS happened a very few years after, my marriage, and is one of those feeling incidents in life that we never forget. My husband's income was moderate, and we found it necessary to deny ourselves many little articles of ornament and luxury, to the end that there might be no serious abatement in the comforts of life. In furnishing our house, we had been obliged to content ourselves mainly with things useful. Our parlor could boast of nine cane-seat chairs; one high-backed cane-seat rocking chair; a pair of card tables; a pair of ottomans, the covers for which I had worked in worsted; and a few illustrated books upon the card tables. There were no pictures on the walls, nor ornaments on the mantle pieces.

For a time after my marriage with Mr. Smith, I did not think much about the plainness of our style of living; but after a while, contracts between my own parlors and those of one or two friends, would take place in my mind; and I often found myself wishing that we could afford a set of candelabras, a pair of china vases, or some choice pieces of Bohemian glass. In fact, I set my heart on something of the kind, though I concealed the weakness from my husband.

Time stole on, and one increase after another to our family, kept up the necessity for careful expenditure, and at no time was there money enough in the purse to justify any outlay beyond what the wants of the household required. So my mantel pieces remained bare as at first, notwithstanding the desire for something to put on them still remained active.

One afternoon, as I sat at work renovating an old garment, with the hope of making it look almost "as good as new," my cook entered and said -

"There's a man down stairs, Mrs. Smith, with a basket full of the most beautiful glass dishes and china ornaments that you ever did see; and he says that he will sell them for old clothes."

"For old clothes?" I responded, but half comprehending what the girl meant.

"Yes ma'am. if you have got an old coat, or a pair of pantaloons that aint good for nothing, he will buy them, and pay you in glass or china."

I paused for a moment to think, and then said -

"Tell him to come up into the dining room, Mary."

The girl went down stairs, and soon came back in company with a dull looking old man, who carried on his arm a large basket, in which were temptingly displayed rich china vases, motto and presentation cups and saucers, glass dishes, and sundry other articles of a like character.

"Any old coats, pantaloons or vests?" said the man, as he placed, carefully, his basket on the floor. "Don't want any money. See here! Beautiful!"

And as he spoke, he took up a pair of vases and held them before my eyes. They were just the thing for my mantle pieces, and I covetted them on the instant.

"What's the price?" I enquired.

"Got an old coat?" was my only answer. "Don't want money."

T. S. Arthur

My husband was the possessor of a coat that had seen pretty good service, and which he had not worn for some time. In fact, it had been voted superannuated, and consigned to a dark corner of the clothes-press. The thought of this garment came very naturally into my mind, and with the thought a pleasant exhilaration of feeling, for I already saw the vases on my mantles.

"Any old clothes?" repeated the vender of china ware.

Without a word I left the dining room, and hurried up to where our large clothes-press stood, in the passage above. From this I soon abstracted the coat, and then descended with quick steps.

The dull face of the old man brightened, the moment his eyes fell upon the garment. He seized it with a nervous movement, and seemed to take in its condition at a single glance. Apparently, the examination was not very satisfactory, for he let the coat fall, in a careless manner, across a chair, giving his shoulders a shrug, while a slight expression of contempt flitted over his countenance.

"Not much good!" fell from his lips after a pause.

By this time I had turned to his basket, and was examining, more carefully, its contents. Most prominent stood the china vases, upon which my heart was already set; and instinctively I took them in my hands.

"What will you give for the coat?" said I.

The old man gave his head a significant shake, as he replied -

"No very good."

"It's worth something," I returned. "Many a poor person would be glad to buy it for a small sum of money. It's only a little defaced. I'm sure its richly worth four or five dollars."

"Pho! Pho! Five dollar! Pho!" The old man seemed angry at my most unreasonable assumption.

"Well, well," said I, beginning to feel a little impatient, "just tell me what you will give for it."

"What you want?" he enquired, his manner visibly changing.

"I want these vases, at any rate," I answered, holding up the articles I had mentioned.

"Worth four, five dollar!" ejaculated the dealer, in well feigned surprise.

I shook my head. He shrugged his shoulders, and commenced searching his basket, from which, after a while, he took a china cup and saucer, on which I read, in gilt letters, "For my Husband."

"Give you this," said he.

It was now my time to show surprise; I answered -

"Indeed you won't, then. But I'll tell you what I will do; I'll let you have the coat for the vases and this cup and saucer."

To this proposition the man gave an instant and decided negative, and seemed half offended by my offer. He threw the coat, which was in his hands again, upon a chair, and stooping down took his basket on his arm. I was deceived by his manner, and began to think that I had proposed rather a hard bargain; so I said -

"You can have the coat for the vases, if you care to make the exchange; if not, why no harm is done."

For the space of nearly half a minute, the old man stood in apparent irresolution, then he replied, as he set down his basket and took out the pair of vases -

"I don't care; you shall have them."

I took the vases and he took the coat. A moment or two more, and I heard the street door close behind the dealer in china ware, with a very decided jar.

"Ain't they beautiful, aunty?" said I to my old aunt Rachel, who had been a silent witness of the scene I have just described; and I held the pair of vases before her eyes.

"Why yes, they are rather pretty, Jane," replied aunt Rachel, a little coldly, as I thought.

"Rather pretty! They are beautiful," said I warmly. "See there!" And I placed them on the dining room mantle. "How much they will improve our parlors."

"Not half so much as that old coat you as good as gave away would have improved the feelings as well as the looks of poor Mr. Bryan, who lives across the street," was the unexpected and rebuking answer of aunt Rachel.

The words smote on my feelings. Mr. Bryan was a poor, but honest and industrious young man, upon whose daily labor a wife and five children were dependent. He went meanly clad, because he could not earn enough, in addition to what his family required, to buy comfortable clothing for himself. I saw, in an instant, what the true disposition of the coat should have been. The china vases would a little improve the appearance of my parlors; but how many pleasant feelings and hours and days of comfort, would the old coat have given to Mr. Bryan. I said no more. Aunt Rachel went on with her knitting, and I took the vases down into the parlors and placed them on the mantles - one in each room. But they looked small, and seemed quite solitary. So I put one on each end of a single mantle. This did better; still, I was disappointed in the appearance they made, and a good deal displeased with myself. I felt that I had made a bad bargain - that is, one from which I should obtain no real pleasure.

For a while I sat opposite the mantle-piece, looking at the vases - but, not admiringly; then I left the parlor, and went about my household duties, but, with a pressure on my feelings. I was far, very far from being satisfied with myself.

About an hour afterwards my husband came home. I did not take him into the parlor to show him my little purchase, for, I had no heart to do so. As we sat at the tea table, he said, addressing me -

"You know that old coat of mine that is up in the clothes-press?"

I nodded my head in assent, but did not venture to speak.

"I've been thinking to-day," added my husband, "that it would be just the thing for Mr. Bryan, who lives opposite. It's rather too much worn for me, but will look quite decent on him, compared with the clothes he now wears. Don't you think it is a good thought? We will, of course, make him a present of the garment."

My eyes drooped to the table, and I felt the blood crimsoning my face. For a moment or two I remained silent, and then answered -

"I'm sorry you didn't think of this before; but it's too late now."

"Too late! Why?" enquired my husband.

"I sold the coat this afternoon," was my reply.

"Sold it!"

"Yes. A man came along with some handsome china ornaments, and I sold the coat for a pair of vases to set on our mantle-pieces."

T. S. Arthur

There was an instant change in my husband's face. He disapproved of what I had done; and, though he uttered no condemning words, his countenance gave too clear an index to his feelings.

"The coat would have done poor Mr. (sic) Byran a great deal more good than the vases will ever do Jane," spoke up aunt Rachel, with less regard for my feelings than was manifested by my husband. "I don't think," she continued, "that any body ought to sell old clothes for either money or nicknackeries to put on the mantle-pieces. Let them be given to the poor, and they'll do some good. There isn't a housekeeper in moderate circumstances that couldn't almost clothe some poor family, by giving away the cast off garments that every year accumulate on her hands."

How sharply did I feel the rebuking spirit in these words of aunt Rachel.

"What's done can't be helped now," said my husband kindly, interrupting, as he spoke, some further remarks that aunt Rachel evidently intended to make. "We must do better next time."

"I must do better," was my quick remark, made in penitent tones. "I was very thoughtless."

To relieve my mind, my husband changed the subject of conversation; but, nothing could relieve the pressure upon my feelings, caused by a too acute consciousness of having done what in the eyes of my husband, looked like a want of true humanity. I could not bear that he should think me void of sympathy for others.

The day following was Sunday. Church time came, and Mr. Smith went to the clothes press for his best coat, which had been worn only for a few months.

"Jane!" he called to me suddenly, in a voice that made me start.

"Jane! Where is my best coat?"

"In the clothes press," I replied, coming out from our chamber into the passage, as I spoke.

"No; it's not here," was his reply. "And, I shouldn't wonder if you had sold my good coat for those china vases."

"No such thing!" I quickly answered, though my heart gave a great bound at his words; and then sunk in my bosom with a low tremor of alarm.

"Here's my old coat," said Mr. Smith, holding up that defaced garment - "Where is the new one?"

"The old clothes man has it, as sure as I live!" burst from my lips.

"Well, that is a nice piece of work, I must confess!"

This was all my husband said; but it was enough to smite me almost to the floor. Covering my face with my hands, I dropped into a chair, and sat and sobbed for a while bitterly.

"It can't be helped now, Jane," said Mr. Smith, at length, in a soothing voice. "The coat is gone, and there is no help for it. You will know better next time."

That was all he said to me then, and I was grateful for his kind consideration. He saw that I was punished quite severely enough, and did not add to my pain by rebuke or complaint.

An attempt was made during the week to recover the coat, valued at some twenty dollars; but the china ornament-man was not to be found - he had made too good a bargain to run the risk of having it broken.

About an hour after the discovery of the loss of my husband's coat, I went quietly down into the parlor, and taking from the

T. S. Arthur

mantle-piece the china vases, worth, probably, a dollar for the pair, concealed them under my apron, lest any one should see what I had; and, returning up stairs, hid them away in a dark closet, where they have ever since remained.

The reader may be sure that I never forgot this, my first and last speculation in china ware.

CHAPTER II

SOMETHING ABOUT COOKS

WAS there ever a good cook who hadn't some prominent fault that completely overshadowed her professional good qualities? If my experience is to answer the question, the reply will be - *no.*

I had been married several years before I was fortunate enough to obtain a cook that could be trusted to boil a potato, or broil a steak. I felt as if completely made up when Margaret served her first dinner. The roast was just right, and all the vegetables were cooked and flavored as well as if I had done it myself - in fact, a little better. My husband eat with a relish not often exhibited, and praised almost every thing on the table.

For a week, one good meal followed another in daily succession. We had hot cakes, light and fine-flavored, every morning for breakfast, with coffee not to be beaten - and chops or steaks steaming from the gridiron, that would have gladdened the heart of an epicure. Dinner was served, during the time, with a punctuality that was rarely a minute at fault, while every article of food brought upon the table, fairly tempted the appetite. Light rolls, rice cakes, or "Sally Luns," made without suggestion on my part usually met us at tea time. In fact, the very delight of Margaret's life appeared to be in cooking. She was born for a cook.

Moreover, strange to say, Margaret was good-tempered, a most

T. S. Arthur

remarkable thing in a good cook; and more remarkable still, was tidy in her person, and cleanly in her work.

"She is a treasure," said I to my husband, one day, as we passed from the dining-room, after having partaken of one of her excellent dinners.

"She's too good," replied Mr. Smith - "too good to last. There must be some bad fault about her - good cooks always have bad faults - and I am looking for its appearance every day."

"Don't talk so, Mr. Smith. There is no reason in the world why a good cook should not be as faultless as any one else."

Even while I said this, certain misgivings intruded themselves. My husband went to his store soon after.

About three o'clock Margaret presented herself, all dressed to go out, and said that she was going to see her sister, but would be back in time to get tea.

She came back, as she promised, but, alas for my good cook! The fault appeared. She was so much intoxicated that, in attempting to lift the kettle from the fire, she let it fall, and came near scalding herself dreadfully. Oh, dear! I shall never forget the sad disappointment of that hour. How the pleasant images of good dinners and comfortable breakfasts and suppers faded from my vision. The old trouble was to come back again, for the faultless cook had manifested a fault that vitiated, for us, all her good qualities.

On the next day, I told Margaret that we must part; but she begged so hard to be kept in her place, and promised good behaviour in future so earnestly, that I was prevailed on to try her again. It was of no use, however - in less than a week she was drunk again, and I had to let her go.

After that, for some months, we had burnt steaks, waxy potatoes, and dried roast beef to our hearts' content; while such luxuries as muffins, hot cakes, and the like were not to be seen on our uninviting table.

My next good cook had such a violent temper, that I was actually afraid to show my face in the kitchen. I bore with her until patience was no longer a virtue, and then she went.

Biddy, who took charge of my "kitchen cabinet," a year or so afterwards, proved herself a culinary artist of no ordinary merit. But, alas! Biddy "kept a room;" and so many strange disappearances of bars of soap, bowls of sugar, prints of butter, etc., took place, that I was forced to the unwilling conclusion that her room was simply a store room for the surplussage of mine. Some pretty strong evidence on this point coming to my mind, I dismissed Biddy, who was particularly forward in declaring her honesty, although I had never accused her of being wanting in that inestimable virtue.

Some of my experiences in cooks have been musing enough. Or, I should rather say, are musing enough to *think* about: they were rather annoying at the time of their occurrence. One of these experiences I will relate. I had obtained a "treasure" in a new cook, who was not only good tempered and cleanly, but understood her business reasonably well. Kitty was a little different from former incumbents of her office in this, that she took an interest in reading, and generally dipped into the morning paper before it found its way up stairs. To this, of course, I had no objection, but was rather pleased to see it. Time, however, which proves all things, showed my cook to be rather too literary in her inclinations. I often found her reading, when it was but reasonable for me to expect that she would be working; and overdone or burnt dishes occasionally marked the degree in which her mind was absorbed in her literary pleasures, which I discovered in time, were not of the highest order-such books as the "Mysteries of Paris" furnishing the aliment that fed her imagination.

"Jane," said my husband to me one morning, as he was about leaving the house, "I believe I must invite my old friend Green to dine with me to-day. He will leave the city to-morrow, and I may not have the pleasure of a social hour with him again for years. Besides, I want to introduce him to you. We were intimate as young men, and much attached to each other. I would like you to know him."

"Invite him, by all means," was my reply.

"I will send home a turkey from market," said Mr. Smith, as he stood holding on to the open door. "Tell Kitty to cook it just right. Mrs. Green, I am told, is a first-rate housekeeper, and I feel like showing you off to the best advantage."

"Don't look for too much," I replied, smiling, "lest you be disappointed."

Mr. Smith went away, and I walked back to the kitchen door to say a word to Kitty. As I looked in, the sound of my feet on the floor caused her to start. She was standing near a window, and at my appearance she hurriedly concealed something under her apron.

"Kitty," said I, "we are to have company to dine with us to-day. Mr. Smith will send home a turkey, which you must dress and cook in the best manner. I will be down during the morning to make some lemon puddings. Be sure to have a good fire in the range, and see that all the drafts are clear."

Kitty promised that every thing should be right, and I went up stairs. In due time the marketing came home. About eleven o'clock I repaired to the kitchen, and, much to my surprise, found all in disorder.

"What in the world have you been doing all the morning?" said I, feeling a little fretted.

Kitty excused herself good naturedly, and commenced bustling about to put things to rights, while I got flour and other articles necessary for my purpose, and went to work at my lemon puddings, which were, in due time, ready for the oven. Giving all necessary directions as to their baking, and charging Kitty to be sure to have every thing on the table precisely at our usual hour for dining, I went up into the nursery to look after the children, and to see about other matters requiring my attention.

Time passed on until, to my surprise, I heard the clock strike one. I had yet to dress for dinner.

"I wonder how Kitty is coming on?" said I to myself. "I hope she will not let the puddings get all dried up."

But, I felt too much in a hurry to go down and satisfy myself as to the state of affairs in the kitchen; and took it for granted that all was right.

A little while afterwards, I perceived an odor as of something burning.

"What is that?" came instinctively from my lips. "If Kitty has let the puddings burn!"

Quick as thought I turned from my room, and went gliding down stairs. As I neared the kitchen, the smell of burned flour, or pastry, grew stronger. All was silent below; and I approached in silence. On entering Kitty's domain, I perceived that lady seated in front of the range, with a brown covered pamphlet novel held close to her face, in the pages of which she was completely lost. I never saw any one more entirely absorbed in a book. No sign of dinner was any where to be seen. Upon the range was a kettle of water boiling over into the fire, and from one of the ovens poured forth a dark smoke, that told too plainly the ruin of my lemon puddings. And, to cap all, the turkey, yet guiltless of fire or dripping pan, was upon the floor, in possession of a strange cat, which had come in through the open window. Bending over the still entranced cook, I read the title of her book. It was "THE WANDERING JEW."

"Kitty!" I don't much wonder, now, at the start she gave, for I presume there was not the zephyr's softness in my voice.

"Oh, ma'am!" She caught her breath as her eyes rested upon the cat and the turkey. "Indeed, ma'am!" And then she made a spring towards puss, who, nimbly eluding her, passed out by the way through which she had come in.

By this time I had jerked open the oven door, when there came rushing out a cloud of smoke, which instantly filled the room. My puddings were burned to a crisp!

As for the turkey, the cat had eaten off one side of the breast, and it was no longer fit for the table.

"Well! this is fine work!" said I, in an angry, yet despairing voice. "Fine work, upon my word!"

"Oh, ma'am!" Kitty interrupted me by saying, "I'll run right off and buy another turkey, and have it cooked in time. Indeed I will, ma'am! And I'll pay for it. It's all my fault! oh dear! dear me! Now don't be angry, Mrs. Smith! I'll have dinner all ready in time, and no one will be any the wiser for this."

"In time!" and I raised my finger towards the kitchen clock, the hands of which marked the period of half past one. Two o'clock was our regular dinner hour.

"Mercy!" ejaculated the frightened cook, as she sank back upon a chair; "I thought it was only a little past eleven. I am sure it was only eleven when I sat down just to read a page or two while the puddings were in the oven!"

The truth was, the "Wandering Jew," in the most exciting portion of which she happened to be, proved too much for her imagination. Her mind had taken no note of time, and two hours passed with the rapidity of a few minutes.

"I don't exactly comprehend this," said my husband, as he sat down with his old friend, to dine off of broiled steak and potatoes, at half-past two o'clock.

"It's all the fault of the, 'Wandering Jew!'" I replied, making an effort to drive away, with a smile, the red signs of mortification that were in my face.

"The Wandering Jew!" returned my husband, looking mystified.

"Yes, the fault lies with that imaginary personage," said I, "strange as it may seem." And then I related the mishaps of the morning. For desert, we had some preserved fruit and cream, and a hearty laugh over the burnt puddings and disfigured turkey.

Poor Kitty couldn't survive the mortification. She never smiled again in my house; and, at the close of the week, removed to another home.

T. S. Arthur

CHAPTER III

LIGHT ON THE SUBJECT

"THE oil's out, mum," said Hannah, the domestic who succeeded Kitty, pushing her head into the room where I sat sewing.

"It can't be," I replied.

"Indade, mum, and it is. There isn't the full of a lamp left," was
the positive answer.

"Then, what have you done with it?" said I, in a firm voice. "It isn't four days since a gallon was sent home from the store."

"Four days! It's more nor a week, mum!"

"Don't tell me that, Hannah," I replied, firmly; "for I know better. I was out on last Monday, and told Brown to send us home a gallon."

"Sure, and it's burned, mum, thin! What else could go with it?"

"It never was burned in our lamps," said I, in answer to this. "You've either wasted it, or given it away."

At this Hannah, as in honor bound, became highly indignant,

and indulged in certain impertinences which I did not feel inclined to notice.

But, as the oil was all gone, and no mistake; and, as the prospect of sitting in darkness was not, by any means, an agreeable one - the only remedy was to order another gallon.

Something was wrong; that was clear. The oil had never been burned.

That evening, myself and husband talked over the matter, and both of us came to the conclusion, that it would never do. The evil must be remedied. A gallon of oil must not again disappear in four days.

"Why," said my husband, "it ought to last us at least a week and a half."

"Not quite so long," I replied. "We burn a gallon a week."

"Not fairly, I'm inclined to think. But four days is out of all conscience."

I readily assented to this, adding some trite remark about the unconscionable wastefulness of domestics.

On the next morning, as my husband arose from bed, he shivered in the chilly air, saying, as he did so:

"That girl's let the fire go out again in the heater! Isn't it too bad? This thing happens now every little while. I'm sure I've said enough to her about it. There's nothing wanted but a little attention."

"It is too bad, indeed," I added.

"There's that fishy smell again!" exclaimed Mr. Smith. "What can it be?"

T. S. Arthur

"Fishy smell! So there is."

"Did you get any mackerel from the store yesterday?"

"None."

"Perhaps Hannah ordered some?"

"No. I had a ham sent home, and told her to have a slice of that broiled for breakfast."

"I don't know what to make of it. Every now and then that same smell comes up through the register - particularly in the morning. I'll bet a sixpence there's some old fish tub in the cellar of which she's made kindling."

"That may be it," said I.

And, for want of a better reason, we agreed, for the time being, upon that hypothesis.

At the end of another four days, word came up that our best sperm oil, for which we paid a dollar and forty cents a gallon, was out again.

"Impossible!" I ejaculated.

"But it is mum," said Hannah. "There's not a scrimption left - not so much as the full of a thimble."

"You must be mistaken. A gallon of oil has never been burned in this house in four days."

"We burned the other gallon in four days," said Hannah, with provoking coolness. "The evenings are very long, and we have a great many lights. There's the parlor light, and the passage light, and the - "

"It's no use for you to talk, Hannah," I replied, interrupting her. "No use in the world. A gallon of oil in four days has never gone by fair means in this house. So don't try to make me believe it - for I won't. I'm too old a housekeeper for that."

Finding that I was not to be convinced, Hannah became angry, and said something about her not being a "thafe." I was unmoved by this, however; and told her, with as much sternness of manner as I could assume, that I should hold her responsible for any future waste of the article; and that if she did not feel inclined to remain on such terms, she had better go.

"Dade, thin, and I'll go to onst," was the girl's spirited answer.

"Very well, Hannah. You are your own mistress in this respect," said I, coolly. "I'm not in the least troubled about filling your place; nor fearful of getting one who will waste a gallon of oil in four days."

Hannah retired from my presence in high indignation, and I fully expected that she would desert my house forthwith. But, no; unlike some others of her class, she knew when she had a good place, and had sense enough to keep it as long as she could stay.

In due time she cooled off, and I heard no more about her getting another place.

"There's that fishy smell again!" exclaimed my husband, as he arose up in bed one morning, a day or two afterwards, and snuffed the air. "And, as I live, the fire in the heater is all out again! I'll have some light on this subject, see if I don't."

And he sprung upon the floor, at the same time hurriedly putting on his dressing gown and a pair of slippers.

"Where are you going?" said I, seeing him moving towards the door.

T. S. Arthur

"To find out where this fishy smell comes from," he replied, disappearing as he spoke.

In about five minutes, Mr. Smith returned.

"Well, if that don't beat all!" he exclaimed, as he re-entered the chamber.

"What?" I very naturally enquired.

"I've found out all about that fishy smell," said he.

"What about it? Where does it come from?"

"You wouldn't guess in a month of Sundays! Well, this is a great world! Live and learn!"

"Explain yourself, Mr. Smith. I'm all impatience."

"I will; and in a few words. The fire was out in the heater."

"Yes."

"And I very naturally took my way down to where I expected to find our lady at work in the re-kindling process."

"Well?"

"Sure enough, there she was, kindling the fire with a vengeance."

"With what?" I asked. "With a vengeance?"

"Yes, with a vengeance to my pocket. She had the oil can in her hands, and was pouring its contents freely into the furnace, in order to quicken combustion. I now understand all about this fishy smell."

"And I all about the remarkable disappearance of a gallon of oil in four days. Kindling the fire with dollar and forty cent oil!"

"Even so!"

"What did you say to her, Mr. Smith?"

"Nothing. But I rather think she'll not want me to look at her again, the huzzy!"

"Kindling fire with my best sperm oil! Well, I can't get over that!"

Something in this wise I continued to ejaculate, now and then, until my astonishment fairly wore itself out.

I didn't consider it worth while to say any thing to Hannah when I went down stairs, thinking it best to let the look my husband spoke of, do its work. By the way, I don't much wonder that she was frightened at his look - for he can - But I forgot - I am speaking of my husband, and he might happen to read this.

Of course, Hannah's days in my house were numbered. No faith was to be placed in a creature who could so shamefully destroy a useful article placed in her hands. If she would burn up the oil, it was but fair to infer that she would as remorselessly make way with other things. So I parted with her. She begged me to let her stay, and made all sorts of promises. But I was immovable.

Whether I bettered myself in the change, is somewhat doubtful.

T. S. Arthur

CHAPTER IV

CHEAP FURNITURE

ONE of the cardinal virtues, at least for housekeepers who are not overburdened in the matter of income, is economy. In the early part of our married life, Mr. Smith and myself were forced to the practice of this virtue, or incur debt, of which both of us had a natural horror. For a few years we lived in the plain style with which we had begun the world. But, when our circumstances improved, we very naturally desired to improve the appearance of things in our household. Our cane seat chairs and ingrain carpet looked less and less attractive every day. And, when we went out to spend an evening, socially, with our friends, the contrast between home and abroad was strikingly apparent to our minds.

"I think," said Mr. Smith to me, one day, "that it is time we re-furnished our parlors."

"If you can afford the outlay," I remarked.

"It won't cost a great deal," he returned.

"Not over three hundred dollars," said I.

Mr. Smith shook his head as he answered: "Half that sum ought to be sufficient. What will we want?"

"A dozen mahogany chairs to begin with," I replied. "There

will be sixty dollars."

"You don't expect to pay five dollars a-piece for chairs?" said my husband, in a tone of surprise.

"I don't think you can get good ones for less."

"Indeed we can. I was looking at a very handsome set yesterday; and the man only asked four dollars for them. I don't in the least doubt that I could get them for three and a half."

"And a dear bargain you would make of that, I do not in the least doubt. It is poor economy, Mr. Smith, to buy cheap furniture. It costs a great deal more in the end, than good furniture, and never gives you any satisfaction."

"But these were good chairs, Jane. As good as I would wish to look at. The man said they were from one of the best shops in the city, and of superior workmanship and finish."

As I make it a point never to prolong an argument with my husband, when I see his mind bent in one direction, I did not urge my view of the case any farther. It was settled, however, that we could afford to re-furnish our parlors in a better style, and that in the course of the coming week, we should go out together and select a Brussels carpet, a sofa, a dozen mahogany chairs, a centre table, &c.

As I had foreseen from the beginning, my husband's ideas of economy were destined to mar everything. At one of the cabinet ware-rooms was a very neat, well-made set of chairs, for which five dollars and a half were asked, but which the dealer, seeing that he was beyond our mark, offered for five dollars. They were cheap at that price. But Mr. Smith could not see that they were a whit better than the set of chairs just mentioned as offered for four dollars; and which he was satisfied could be bought for three and a half. So I went with him to look at them. They proved to be showy enough, if that

T. S. Arthur

were any recommendation, but had a common look in my eyes. They were not to be compared with the set we had just been examining.

"Now, are they not very beautiful, Jane?" said my husband. "To me they are quite as handsome as those we were asked sixty dollars for."

From this I could not but dissent, seeing which, the cunning dealer came quickly to my husband's side of the question with various convincing arguments, among the strongest of which was an abatement in the price of the chairs - he seeing it to be for his interest to offer them for three dollars and three-quarters a-piece.

"I'll give you three and a-half," said Mr. Smith, promptly.

"Too little, that, sir," returned the dealer. "I don't make a cent on them at three and three-quarters. They are fully equal, in every respect, to the chairs you were offered at five dollars. I know the manufacturer, and have had his articles often."

"Say three and a-half, and it's a bargain," was the only reply made to this by my economical husband.

I was greatly in hopes that the man would decline this offer; but, was disappointed. He hesitated for some time, and, at last, said:

"Well, I don't care, take them along; though it is throwing them away. Such a bargain you will never get again, if you live to be as old as Mathuselah. But, now, don't you want something else? I can sell you cheaper and better articles in the furniture line than you can get in the city. Small profits and quick sales - I go in for the nimble sixpence."

My husband was in the sphere of attraction, and I saw that it would take a stronger effort on my part to draw him out than I wished to make. So, I yielded with as good a grace as possible, and aided in the selection of a cheap sofa, a cheap, overgrown centre table, and two or three other article that were almost "thrown away."

Well, our parlor was furnished with its new dress in good time, and made quite a respectable appearance. Mr. Smith was delighted with everything; the more particularly as the cost had been so moderate. I had my own thoughts on the subject; and looked very confidently for some evidences of imperfection in our great bargains. I was not very long kept in suspense. One morning, about two weeks after all had been fitted out so elegantly, while engaged in dusting the chairs, a part of the mahogany ornament in the back of one of them fell off. On the next day, another showed the same evidence of imperfect workmanship. A few evenings afterwards, as we sat at the centre table, one of our children leaned on it rather heavily, when there was a sudden crack, and the side upon which he was bearing his weight, swayed down the distance of half an inch or more. The next untoward event was the dropping of one of its feet by the sofa, and the warping up of a large piece of veneering on the back. While lamenting over this, we discovered a broken spring ready to make its way through the hair cloth covering.

"So much for cheap furniture," said I, in a tone of involuntary triumph.

My husband looked at me half reproachfully, and so I said no more.

It was now needful to send for a cabinet maker, and submit our sofa and chairs to his handy workmanship. He quickly discovered other imperfections, and gave us the consoling information that our fine furniture was little above fourth-rate in quality, and dear at any price. A ten dollar bill was required to pay the damage they had already sustained, even under our careful hands.

A more striking evidence of our folly in buying cheap furniture

T. S. Arthur

was, however, yet to come. An intimate friend came in one evening to sit a few hours with us. After conversing for a time, both he and my husband took up books, and commenced reading, while I availed myself of the opportunity to write a brief letter. Our visitor, who was a pretty stout man, had the bad fault of leaning back in his chair, and balancing himself on its hind legs; an experiment most trying to the best (sic) mahogahy chairs that were ever made.

We were all sitting around the centre table, upon which burned a tall astral lamp, and I was getting absorbed in my letter, when suddenly there was a loud crash, followed by the breaking of the table from its centre, and the pitching over of the astral lamp, which, in falling, just grazed my side, and went down, oil and all, upon our new carpet! An instant more, and we were in total darkness. But, ere the light went out, a glance had revealed a scene that I shall never forget. Our visitor, whose weight, as he tried his usual balancing experiment, had caused the slender legs of his chair to snap off short, had fallen backwards. In trying to save himself, he had caught at the table, and wrenched that from its centre fastening. Startled by this sudden catastrophe, my husband had sprung to his feet, grasping his chair with the intent of drawing it away, when the top of the back came off in his hand. I saw all this at a single glance - and then we were shrouded in darkness.

Of the scene that followed, I will not speak. My lady readers can, (sic) witout any effort of the mind, imagine something of its unpleasant reality. As for our visitor, when lights were brought in, he was no where to be seen. I have a faint recollection of having heard the street door shut amid the confusion that succeeded the incident just described.

About a week afterwards, the whole of our cheap furniture was sent to auction, where it brought less than half its first cost. It was then replaced with good articles, by good workmen, at a fair price; not one of which has cost us, to this day, a single cent for repairs.

A housekeeping friend of mine, committed, not, long since, a similar error. Her husband could spare her a couple of hundred dollars for re-furnishing purposes; but, as his business absorbed nearly all of his time and thoughts, he left with her the selection of the new articles that were to beautify their parlors and chambers, merely saying to her:

"Let what you get be good. It is cheapest in the end."

Well, my friend had set her heart on a dozen chairs, a new sofa, centre table, and "what-not," for her parlors; and on a dressing-bureau, mahogany bedstead, and wash-stand, for her chamber, besides a new chamber carpet. Her first visit was to the ware-rooms of one of our best cabinet makers; but, his prices completely frightened her - for, at his rate, the articles she wanted would amount to more than all the money she had to spend, and leave nothing for the new chamber carpet.

"I must buy cheaper," said she.

"The cheapest is generally dearest in the end," returned the cabinet maker.

"I don't know about that," remarked the lady, whose thoughts did not take in the meaning of the man's words. "All I know is, that I can get as good articles as I desire at lower prices than you ask."

It did not once occur to my friend, that it would be wisest to lessen the number of articles, and get the remainder of the first quality. No; her heart covered the whole inventory at first made out, and nothing less would answer. So she went to an auction store, and bought inferior articles at lower prices. I visited her soon after. She showed me her bargains, and, with an air of exultation, spoke of the cost.

"What do you think I paid for this?" said she, referring to a showy dressing-bureau; and, as she spoke, she took hold of the suspended looking-glass, and moved the upper portion of it forward. "Only seventeen dollars!"

The words had scarcely passed her lips, ere the looking-glass broke away from one of the screws that held it in the standards, and fell, crashing, at our feet!

It cost just seven dollars to replace the glass. But, that was not all - over thirty dollars were paid during the first year for repairs. And this is only the beginning of troubles.

Cheap furniture is, in most cases, the dearest that housekeepers can buy. It is always breaking, and usually costs more, in a year or two, than the difference between its price and that of first-rate articles; to say nothing of the vexation and want of satisfaction that always attends its possession. Better be content with fewer articles, if the purse be low, and have them good.

While on this subject, I will incorporate in these "Confessions" an "Experience" of my sister and her husband, Mr. and Mrs. John Jones. Mr. Jones is, in some respects, very much like Mr. Smith, and, as will be seen in the story about to be given, my sister's ideas of things and my own, run quite parallel to each other. The story has found its way, elsewhere, into print, for Mr. Jones, like myself, has a natural fondness for types. But its repetition here will do no harm, and bring it before many who would not otherwise see it.

CHAPTER V

IS IT ECONOMY?

THE "Experience" of my relative, Mr. John Jones, referred to in the preceding chapter, is given in what follows. After reading it, we think that few young housekeepers will commit the folly of indulging to any very great extent in cheap furniture.

We had been married five years, and during the time had boarded for economy's sake. But the addition of one after another to our family, admonished us that it was getting time to enlarge our borders; and so we were determined to go to housekeeping. In matters of domestic economy both my wife and myself were a little "green," but I think that I was the greenest of the two.

To get a house was our first concern, and to select furniture was our next. The house was found after two months' diligent search, and at the expense of a good deal of precious shoe leather. Save me from another siege at house-hunting! I would about as soon undertake to build a suitable dwelling with my own hands, as to find one "exactly the thing" already up, and waiting with open doors for a tenant. All the really desirable houses that we found ticketed "to let," were at least two prices above our limit, and most of those within our means we would hardly have lived in rent free.

At last, however, we found a cosey little nest of a house, just

T. S. Arthur

built, and clean and neat as a new pin, from top to bottom. It suited us to a T. And now came the next most important business - selecting furniture. My wife's ideas had always been a little in advance of mine. That is, she liked to have every thing of the best quality; and had the weakness, so to speak, of desiring to make an appearance. As my income, at the time, was but moderate, and the prospect of an increase thereof not very flattering, I felt like being exceedingly prudent in all outlays for furniture.

"We must be content with things few and plain," said I, as we sat down one morning to figure up what we must get.

"But let them be good," said my wife.

"Strong and substantial," was my reply. "But we can't afford to pay for much extra polish and (sic) filagree work."

"I don't want any thing very extra, Mr. Jones," returned my wife, a little uneasily. "Though what I do have, I would like good. It's no economy, in the end, to buy cheap things."

The emphasis on the word cheap, rather grated on my ear; for I was in favor of getting every thing as cheap as possible.

"What kind of chairs did you think of getting?" asked Mrs. Jones.

"A handsome set of cane-seat," I replied, thinking that in this, at least, I would be even with her ideas on the subject of parlor chairs. But her face did not brighten.

"What would you like?" said I.

"I believe it would be more economical in the end to get good stuffed seat, mahogany chairs," replied Mrs. Jones.

"At five dollars a-piece, Ellen?"

"Yes. Even at five dollars a-piece. They would last us our life-time; while cane-seat chairs, if we get them, will have to be renewed two or three times, and cost a great deal more in the end, without being half so comfortable, or looking half-so well."

"Sixty dollars for a dozen chairs, when very good ones can be had for twenty-four dollars! Indeed, Ellen, we mustn't think of such a thing. We can't afford it. Remember, there are a great many other things to buy."

"I know, dear; but I am sure it will be much more economical in the end for us to diminish the number of articles, and add to the quality of what we do have. I am very much like the poor woman who preferred a cup of clear, strong, fragrant coffee, three times a week, to a decoction of burnt rye every day. What I have, I do like good."

"And so do I, Ellen. But, as I said before, there will be, diminish as we may, a great many things to buy, and we must make the cost of each as small as possible. We must not think of such extravagance as mahogany chairs now. At some other time we may get them."

My wife here gave up the point, and, what I thought a little remarkable, made no more points on the subject of furniture. I had every thing my own way; I bought cheap to my heart's content. It was only necessary for me to express my approval of an article, for her to assent to its purchase.

As to patronizing your fashionable cabinet makers and high-priced upholsterers, we were not guilty of the folly, but bought at reasonable rates from auction stores and at public sales. Our parlor carpets cost but ninety cents a yard, and were handsomer than those for which a lady of our acquaintance. paid a dollar and thirty-eight. Our chairs were of a neat, fancy pattern, and had cost thirty dollars a dozen. We had hesitated for some time between a set at twenty-four dollars a dozen and these; but the style being so much more attractive, we let our taste govern in the selection. The price of our sofa was eighteen dollars, and I thought it a really genteel affair, though my wife was not in raptures about it. A pair of card tables for fifteen dollars, and a marble-top centre table for fourteen, gave our parlors quite a handsome appearance.

"I wouldn't ask any thing more comfortable or genteel than this," said, I, when the parlors were all "fixed" right.

Mrs. Jones looked pleased with the appearance of things, but did not express herself extravagantly.

In selecting our chamber furniture, a handsome dressing-bureau and French bedstead that my wife went to look at in the ware-room of a high-priced cabinet maker, tempted her strongly, and it was with some difficulty that I could get her ideas back to a regular maple four-poster, a plain, ten dollar bureau, and a two dollar dressing-glass. Twenty and thirty dollar mattresses, too, were in her mind, but when articles of the kind, just as good to wear, could be had at eight and ten dollars, where was the use of wasting money in going higher?

The ratio of cost set down against the foregoing articles, was maintained from garret to kitchen; and I was agreeably disappointed to find, after the last bill for purchases was paid, that I was within the limit of expenditures I had proposed to make by over a hundred dollars.

The change from a boarding-house to a comfortable home was, indeed, pleasant. We could never get done talking about it. Every thing was so quiet, so new, so clean, and so orderly.

"This is living," would drop from our lips a dozen times a week.

One day, about three months after we had commenced housekeeping, I came home, and, on entering the parlor, the first thing that met my eyes was a large spot of white on the new sofa. A piece of the veneering had been knocked off, completely disfiguring it.

"What did that?" I asked of my wife.

"In setting back a chair that I had dusted," she replied, "one of the feet touched the sofa lightly, when off dropped that veneer like a loose flake. I've been examining the sofa since, and find that it is a very bad piece of work. Just look here."

And she drew me over to the place where my eighteen dollar sofa stood, and pointed out sundry large seams that had gaped open, loose spots in the veneering, and rickety joints. I saw now, what I had not before seen, that the whole article was of exceedingly common material and common workmanship.

"A miserable piece of furniture!" said I.

"It is, indeed," returned Mrs. Jones. "To buy an article like this, is little better than throwing money into the street."

For a month the disfigured sofa remained in the parlor, a perfect eye-sore, when another piece of the veneering sloughed off, and one of the feet became loose. It was then sent to a cabinet maker for repair; and cost for removing and mending just five dollars.

Not long after this, the bureau had to take a like journey, for it had, strangely enough, fallen into sudden dilapidation. All the locks were out of order, half the knobs were off, there was not a drawer that didn't require the most accurate balancing of forces in order to get it shut after it was once open, and it showed premonitory symptoms of shedding its skin like a snake. A five dollar bill was expended in putting this into something like *usable* order and respectable aspect. By this time a new set of castors was needed for the maple four-poster, which was obtained at the expense of two dollars. Moreover, the head-board to said four-poster, which, from its exceeding ugliness, had, from the first, been a terrible eye-sore to Mrs. Jones, as well as to myself, was, about this period, removed,

T. S. Arthur

and one of more sightly appearance substituted, at the additional charge of six dollars. No tester frame had accompanied the cheap bedstead at its original purchase, and now my wife wished to have one, and also a light curtain above and valance below. All these, with trimmings, etc., to match, cost the round sum of ten dollars.

"It looks very neat," said Mrs. Jones, after her curtains were up.

"It does, indeed," said I.

"Still," returned Mrs. Jones, "I would much rather have had a handsome mahogany French bedstead."

"So would I," was my answer. "But you know they cost some thirty dollars, and we paid but sixteen for this."

"Sixteen!" said my wife, turning quickly toward me. "It cost more than that."

"Oh, no. I have the bill in my desk," was my confident answer.

"Sixteen was originally paid, I know," said Mrs. Jones. "But then, remember, what it has cost since. Two dollars for castors, six for a new head-board, and ten for tester and curtains. Thirty-four dollars in all; when a very handsome French bedstead, of good workmanship, can be bought for thirty dollars."

I must own that I was taken somewhat aback by this array of figures "that don't lie."

"And for twenty dollars we could have bought a neat, well made dressing-bureau, at Moore and Campion's, that would have lasted for twice as many years, and always looked in credit."

"But ours, you know, only cost ten," said I.

"The bureau, such as it is, cost ten, and the glass two. Add five that we have already paid for repairs, and the four that our maple bedstead has cost above the price of a handsome French, one, and we will have the sum of twenty-one dollars, - enough to purchase as handsome a dressing-bureau as I would ask. So you see. Mr. Jones, that our cheap furniture is not going to turn out so cheap after all. And as for looks, why no one can say there is much to brag of."

This was a new view of the case, and certainly one not very flattering to my economical vanity. I gave in, of course, and, admitted that Mrs. Jones was right.

But the dilapidations and expenses for repairs, to which I have just referred, were but as the "beginning of sorrows." It took, about three years to show the full fruits of my error. By the end of that time, half my parlor chairs had been rendered useless in consequence of the back-breaking and seat-rending ordeals through which they had been called to pass. The sofa was unanimously condemned to the dining room, and the ninety cent carpet had gone on fading and defacing, until my wife said she was ashamed to put it even on her chambers. For repairs, our furniture had cost, up to this period, to say nothing of the perpetual annoyance of having it put out of order, and running for the cabinet maker and upholsterer, not less than a couple of hundred dollars.

Finally, I grew desperate.

"I'll have decent, well made furniture, let it cost what it will," said I, to Mrs. Jones.

"You will find it cheapest in the end," was her quiet reply.

On the next day we went to a cabinet maker, whose reputation for good work stood among the highest in the city; and ordered new parlor and chamber furniture - mahogany chairs, French bedstead, dressing-bureau and all, and as soon as they came home, cleared the house of all the old cheap (dear!) trash

T. S. Arthur

with which we had been worried since the day we commenced housekeeping

A good many years have passed since, and we have not paid the first five dollar bill for repairs. All the drawers run as smoothly as railroad cars; knobs are tight; locks in prime order, and veneers cling as tightly to their places as if they had grown there. All is right and tight, and wears an orderly, genteel appearance; and what is best of all the cost of every thing we have, good as it is, is far below the *real* cost of what is inferior.

"It is better - much better," said I to Mrs. Jones, the other day.

"Better!" was her reply. "Yes, indeed, a thousand times better to have good things at once. Cheap furniture is dearest in the end. Every housekeeper ought to know this in the beginning. If we had known it, see what we would have saved."

"If *I* had known it, you mean," said I.

My wife looked kindly, not triumphantly, into my face, and smiled. When she again spoke, it was on another subject.

CHAPTER VI

LIVING AT A CONVENIENT DISTANCE

THERE are few of us who do not feel, at some time in life, the desire for change. Indeed, change of place corresponding, as it does, in outward nature, to change of state in the mind, it is not at all surprising that we should, now and then, feel a strong desire to remove from the old, and get into new locations, and amid different external associations. Thus, we find, in many families, an ever recurring tendency to removal. Indeed, I have some housekeeping friends who are rarely to be found in the same house, or in the same part of the city, in any two consecutive years. Three moves, Franklin used to say, were equal to a fire. There are some to whom I could point, who have been, if this holds true, as good as burned out, three or four times in the last ten years.

But, I must not write too long a preface to my present story. Mr. Smith and myself cannot boast of larger organs of Inhabitativeness - I believe, that is the word used by phrenologists - than many of our neighbors. Occasionally we have felt dissatisfied with the state of things around us, and become possessed of the demon of change. We have moved quite frequently, sometimes attaining superior comfort, and some times, getting rather the worst of, it for "the change."

A few years ago, in the early spring-time, Mr. Smith said to me, one day:

"I noticed, in riding out yesterday, a very pleasant country house on the Frankford Road, to let, and it struck me that it would be a fine thing for us, both as to health and comfort, to rent it for the summer season. What do you think of it?"

"I always, loved the country, you know," was my response.

My heart had leaped at the proposition.

"It is such a convenient distance from the city," said Mr. Smith.

"How far?"

"About four miles."

"Do the stages pass frequently?"

"Every half hour; and the fare is only twelve and a half cents."

"So low! That is certainly an inducement."

"Yes, it is. Suppose we go out and look at the house?"

"Very well," said I. And then we talked over the pleasures and advantage that would result from a residence in the country, at such a convenient distance from the city.

On the next day we went to look at the place, and found much, both in the house and grounds, to attract us. There was a fine shaded lawn, and garden with a stock of small and large fruit.

"What a delightful place for the children," I exclaimed.

"And at such a convenient distance from the city," said my husband. "I can go in and out to business, and scarcely miss the time. But do you think you would like the country?"

"O, yes. I've always loved the country."

"We can move back into the city when the summer closes," said Mr. Smith.

"Why not remain here permanently? It will be too expensive to keep both a city and country house," I returned.

"It will be too dreary through the winter."

"I don't think so. I always feel cheerful in the country. And, then, you know, the house is at such a convenient distance, and the stages pass the door at every half hour. You can get to business as easily as if we resided in the city."

I was in the mood for a change, and so it happened was Mr. Smith. The more we thought and talked about the matters, the more inclined were we to break up in the city, and go permanently to the country. And, finally, we resolved to try the experiment.

So the pleasant country house was taken, and the town house given up, and, in due time, we took our flight to where nature had just carpeted the earth in freshest green, and caused the buds to expand, and the trees of the forest to clothe themselves in verdure.

How pleasant was every thing. A gardener had been employed to put the garden and lawn in order, and soon we were delighted to see the first shoots from seeds that had been planted, making their way through the ground. To me, all was delightful. I felt almost as light-hearted as a child, and never tired of expressing my pleasure at the change.

"Come and see us," said I, to one city friend and another, on meeting them. "We're in a most delightful place, and at such a convenient distance from the city. Just get into the Frankford omnibus, which starts from Hall's, in Second street above Market, every half hour, and you will come to our very door.

T. S. Arthur

And I shall be so delighted to have a visit from you."

In moving from the city, I took with me two good domestics, who had lived in my family for over a year. Each had expressed herself as delighted at the prospect of getting into the country, and I was delighted to think they were so well satisfied, for I had feared lest they would be disinclined to accompany us.

About a month after our removal, one of them, who had looked dissatisfied about something, came to me and said:

"I want to go back to the city, Mrs. Smith; I don't like living in the country."

"Very well," I replied. "You must do as you please. But I thought you preferred this to the city?"

"I thought I would like it, but I don't. It's too lonesome."

I did not persuade her to stay. That error I had once or twice, ere this, fallen into, and learned to avoid it in future. So she went back to the city, and I was left with but a single girl. Three days only elapsed before this one announced her intended departure.

"But you will stay," said I, "until I can get some one in your place."

"My week will be up on Saturday," was replied. "Can you get a girl by that time?"

"That leaves me only two days, Mary; I'm afraid not."

Mary looked unamiable enough at this answer. We said no more to each other. In the afternoon I went to the city to find a new domestic, if possible, but returned unsuccessful.

Saturday came, and to my surprise and trouble, Mary persisted in going away. So I was left, with my family of six persons, without any domestic at all.

Sunday proved to me any thing but a day of rest. After washing and dressing the children, preparing breakfast, clearing away the table, making the beds, and putting the house to order, I set about getting dinner. This meal furnished and eaten, and the dishes washed and put away, I found myself not only completely tired out, but suffering from a most dreadful headache. I was lying down, about four o'clock, in a half-waking and sleeping state, with my head a little easier, when my husband, who was sitting by the window, exclaimed:

"If there isn't Mr. and Mrs. Peters and their three children, getting out of the stage!"

"Not coming here!" said I, starting up in bed, while, at the same moment, my headache returned with a throbbing intensity that almost blinded me.

"Yes, coming here," replied Mr. Smith.

"How unfortunate!" came from my lips, as I clasped my hands to my temples.

Now, Mr. and Mrs. Peters were people for whom we had no particular friendship. We visited each other scarcely once a year, and had never reciprocated an evening to tea. True, I had, on the occasion of meeting Mrs. Peters, about a week before, while stopping in the city, said to her, while praising my new country home:

"You must come and see me sometime during the summer."

The invitation was intended as a compliment more than anything else. I didn't particularly care about a visit from her; and certainly had no idea that she would take me at my word. So much for insincerity.

"Go down and ask them into the parlor," said I to Mr. Smith.

T. S. Arthur

"I will dress myself and join you in a little while."

In about half an hour I left my room, feeling really quite unwell. I found my visitors walking in the garden, and their children ranging about like wild colts, to the particular detriment of choice shrubbery and garden beds.

"Oh, what a delightful place!" exclaimed Mrs. Peters, on my meeting her. "I really envy you! You see that I have accepted your very kind invitation. I said to my husband to-day, says I, wouldn't it be nice to make the Smiths a visit this afternoon. They live at such a convenient distance; and it will be such a treat to the children. Well, just as you like, said Mr. Peters. And so, as soon as dinner was over, we got ready and came out. Oh, I'm delighted! What a sweet spot you have chosen. I shall come and see you often."

And thus she (sic) run on, while I smiled, and responded with all due politeness, and to a certain extent, hypocritical pretence of pleasure at the visit.

They had come to spend the afternoon, and take tea with us, of course, and, as the last stage went by at seven o'clock, I was soon under the necessity of leaving my guests, in order to engage in certain preliminary acts that looked towards an early supper. Oh, how my head did throb; and with what an effort did I drag my weary feet about!

But, the longest trial - the most painful ordeal has an end; and the end of this came at length. Our visitors, after spending a few hours, and being served with tea, took their departure, assuring us, as they did so, that they had spent a delightful afternoon, and would be certain to come again soon.

In ten minutes after they had left the house, I was in bed.

Two whole weeks elapsed before I succeeded in getting a girl; and six times during that period, we had friends out from the city to take tea with us; and one young lady spent three whole days!

When the season of fruits came, as we had a few apple and pear trees, besides a strawberry bed, and a fine row of raspberry bushes, our city friends, especially those who had children, were even more particular in their attentions. Our own children, we could make understand the propriety of leaving the small fruit to be picked for table use, so that all could share in its enjoyment. But, visitors' children comprehended nothing of this, and rifled our beds and bushes so constantly, that, although they would have given our table a fair supply of berries, in the season, we never once could get enough to be worth using, and so were forced to purchase our fruit in the city.

After a destructive visitation of this nature, during strawberry time, I said to Mr. Smith, as he was leaving for the city one morning -

"I wish you would take a small basket with you, and bring out two or three quarts of strawberries for tea. I've only tasted them once or twice, and it's hopeless to think of getting any from our garden."

Well, when Mr. Smith came home with his two or three quarts of strawberries, we had six women and children, visitors from the city, to partake of them. Of course, our own children, who had been promised strawberries at tea time, and who had been looking for them, did'nt get a taste.

And thus it happened over and over again.

As the weather grew warmer and warmer, particular friends whom we were glad to see, and friends, so called, into whose houses we had rarely, if ever ventured, came out to get a "mouthful of fresh air," and to "see something green." We lived at "such a convenient distance," that it was no trouble at all to run out and look at us.

T. S. Arthur

Twice again during the summer, I was left without a single domestic. Girls didn't like to leave the city, where they had been used to meeting their acquaintances every few days; and, therefore, it was hard to retain them. So it went on.

I had poor help, and was overrun with company, at such a rate, that I was completely worn out. I rarely heard the rumble of the approaching stage that I did not get nervous.

Early in August, Mr. Smith said to me, one evening after returning from the city - on that very morning, a family of four had left me, after staying three days -

"I met Mr. Gray this afternoon, and he told me that they were coming out to see you to-morrow. That he was going away for a while, and his wife thought that it would be such a pleasant time to redeem her promise of making you a visit."

"Oh dear! What next!" I exclaimed in a distressed voice. "Is there to be no end to this?"

"Not before frost, I presume," returned Mr. Smith, meaningly.

"I wish frost would come along quickly, then," was my response. "But how long is Mr. Gray going to be absent from home?"

"He didn't say."

"And we're to have his whole family, I suppose, during his absence."

"Doubtless."

"Well, I call that taxing hospitality and good feeling a little too far. I don't want them here! I've no room for them without inconvenience to ourselves. Besides, my help is poor."

But, all my feelings of repugnance were of no avail. As I was sitting, on the next day, by a window, that overlooked the road, I saw the stage draw up, and issue therefrom Mr. Jones, Mrs. Jones, servant and five children - two of the latter twin-babies. They had boxes, carpet bags, bundles, &c., indicating a prolonged sojourn, and one little boy dragged after him a pet dog, that came also to honor us with a visit.

Down to meet them at the door, with as good a grace as possible, I hurried. Words of welcome and pleasure were on my tongue, though I am not sure that my face did not belie my utterance. But, they were all too pleased to get into our snug country quarters, to perceive any drawback in their reception.

I will not describe my experience during the next three weeks - for, Mr. Gray took the tour of the Lakes before returning, and was gone full three weeks, leaving his family to our care for the whole time.

"Heaven be praised, that is over!" was my exclamation, when I saw the stage move off that bore them from our door.

Frost at length came, and with it expired the visiting season. We were still at a convenient distance from the city; but, our friends, all at once, seemed to have forgotten us.

"You are not going to move back, now," said a friend in surprise, to whom I mentioned in the following March our intention to return to the city.

"Yes," I replied.

"Just as spring is about opening? Why, surely, after passing the dreary winter in the country, you will not come to the hot and dusty town to spend the summer? You are at such a convenient distance too; and your friends can visit you so easily."

Yes, the distance was convenient; and we had learned to appreciate that advantage. But back to the city we removed;

T. S. Arthur

and, when next we venture to the country, will take good care to get beyond a convenient distance.

CHAPTER VII

THE PICKED-UP DINNER

IT was "washing day;" that day of all days in the week most dreaded by housekeepers. We had a poor breakfast, of course. Cook had to help with the washing, and, as washing was the important thing for the day, every thing else was doomed to suffer. The wash kettle was to her of greater moment than the tea kettle or coffee pot; and the boiling of wash water first in consideration, compared with broiling the steak.

The breakfast bell rung nearly half an hour later than usual. As I entered the dining room, I saw that nearly every thing was in disorder, and that the table was little over half set. Scarcely had I taken my seat, ere the bell was in my hand.

"There's no sugar on the table, Kitty."

These were my words, as the girl entered, in obedience to my summons.

"Oh, I forgot!" she ejaculated, and hurriedly supplied the deficiency.

Ting-a-ling-a-ling, went my bell, ere she had reached the kitchen.

"There's no knife and fork for the steak," said I, as Kitty re-appeared.

The knife and fork were furnished, but not with a very amiable grace.

"What's the matter with this coffee?" asked Mr. Smith, after sipping a spoonful or two. "It's got a queer taste."

"I'm sure I don't know."

It was plain that I was going to have another trying day; and I began to feel a little worried. My reply was not, therefore, made in a very composed voice.

Mr. Smith continued to sip his coffee with a spoon, and to taste the liquid doubtingly. At length he pushed his cup from him, saying:

"It's no use; I can't drink that! I wish you would just taste it. I do believe Kitty has dropped a piece of soap into the coffee pot."

By this time I had turned out a cup of the fluid for myself, and proceeded to try its quality. It certainly had a queer taste; but, as to the substance to which it was indebted for its peculiar flavor, I was in total ignorance. My husband insisted that it was soap. I thought differently; but we made no argument on the subject.

The steak was found, on trial, to be burned so badly that it was not fit to be eaten. And my husband had to make his meal of bread and butter and cold water. As for myself, this spoiling of our breakfast for no good reason, completely destroyed both my appetite and my temper.

"You'd better get your dinner at an eating house, Mr. Smith," said I, as he arose from the table. "It's washing day, and we shall have nothing comfortable."

"Things will be no more comfortable for you than for me," was kindly replied by my husband.

"We shall only have a picked-up dinner," said I.

"I like a good picked-up dinner," answered Mr. Smith. "There is something so out of the ordinary routine of ribs, loins, and sirloins - something so comfortable and independent about it. No, you cannot eat your picked-up dinner alone."

"Drop the word *good* from your description, and the picked-up dinner will be altogether another affair," said I. "No, don't come home to-day, if you please; for every thing promises to be most uncomfortable. Get yourself a good dinner at an eating house, and leave me to go through the day as well as I can."

"And you are really in earnest?" said my husband, seriously.

"I certainly am," was my reply. "Entirely in earnest. So, just oblige me by not coming home to dinner."

Mr. Smith promised; and there was so much off of my mind. I could not let him come home without seeing that he had a good dinner. But, almost any thing would do for me and the children.

In some things, I am compelled to say that my husband is a little uncertain. His memory is not always to be depended on. Deeply absorbed in business, as he was at that time, he frequently let things of minor importance pass from his thoughts altogether.

So it happened on the present occasion. He forgot that it was washing day, and that he had promised to dine down town. Punctually at half-past one he left his place of business, as usual, and took his way homeward. As he walked along, he met an old friend who lived in a neighboring town, and who was on a visit to our city.

"Why, Mr. Jones! How glad I am to see you! When did you arrive?"

T. S. Arthur

And my husband grasped the hand of his friend eagerly.

"Came in last evening," replied Mr. Jones. "How well you look, Smith! How is your family?"

"Well - very well. When do you leave?"

"By this afternoon's line."

"So soon? You make no stay at all?"

"I came on business, and must go back again with as little delay as possible."

"Then you must go and dine with me, Jones. I won't take no for an answer. Want to have a long talk with you about old times."

"Thank you, Mr. Smith," replied Jones. "But, as I don't happen to know your good lady, I hardly feel free to accept your invitation."

"Don't hesitate for that. She'll be delighted to see you. Always glad to meet any of my old friends. So come along. I've a dozen things to say to you."

"I'm really afraid of intruding on your wife," said Mr. Jones, still holding back from the invitation.

"Nonsense!" answered my husband. "My friends are hers. She will be delighted to see you. I've talked of you to her a hundred times."

At this Mr. Jones yielded.

"I can't promise you any thing extra," said Mr. Smith, as they walked along. "Nothing more than a good, plain family dinner, and a warm welcome."

"All I could ask or desire," returned Mr. Jones.

It was a few minutes to two o'clock. The bell had rung for dinner; and I was just rising to go to the dining room, when I heard the street door open, and the sound of my husband's voice in the passage. There was a man in company with him, for I distinctly heard the tread of a pair of feet. What could this mean? I remained seated, listening with attention.

My husband entered the parlor with his companion, talking in a cheerful, animated strain; and I heard him pull up the blinds and throw open the shutters. Presently he came tripping lightly up the stairs to my sitting room.

"I've brought a friend home to dinner, Jane," said he, as coolly and as confidently as if it were not washing day; and as if he had not told me on going out, that he would dine at an eating house.

This was a little too much for my patience and forbearance.

"Are you beside yourself, Mr. Smith?" I replied, my face instantly becoming flushed, and my eyes glancing out upon him the sudden indignation I felt at such treatment.

"Why, Jane! Jane! This is not kind in you," said my husband, with regret and displeasure in his voice. "It is rather hard if a man can't ask an old friend home to dine with him once in five years, without asking the special permission of his wife."

"Mr. Smith! Are you not aware that this is washing day?"

There was an instant change in my husband's countenance. He seemed bewildered for a few moments.

"And, moreover," I continued, "are you not aware that I was to have a picked-up dinner at home, and that you were to dine at an eating house?"

T. S. Arthur

"I declare!" Mr. Smith struck his hands together, and turned around once upon his heel. - "I entirely forgot about that."

"What's to be done?" said I, almost crying with vexation. "I've nothing for dinner but fried ham and eggs."

"The best we can do is the best," returned Mr. Smith. "You can give Mr. Jones a hearty welcome, and that will compensate for any defects in the dinner. I forewarned him that we should not entertain him very sumptuously."

"You'd better tell him the whole truth at once," said I, in answer to this; "and then take him to an eating house."

But my good husband would hear to nothing of this. He had invited his old friend to dine with him; and dine he must, if it was only on a piece of dry bread.

"Pick up something. Do the best you can," he returned. "We can wait for half an hour."

"I've nothing in the house, I tell you," was my answer made in no very pleasant tones; for I felt very much irritated and outraged by my husband's thoughtless conduct.

"There, there, Jane. Don't get excited about the matter," said he soothingly. But his words were not like oil to the troubled waters of my spirit.

"I am excited," was my response. "How can I help being so? It is too much! You should have had more consideration."

But, talking was of no use. Mr. Jones was in the parlor, and had come to take a family dinner with us. So, nothing was left but to put a good face on the matter; or, at least, to try and do so.

"Dinner's on the table now," said I. "All is there that we can have to-day. So just invite your friend to the dining room, where you will find me."

So saying, I took a little fellow by the hand, who always eat with us, and led him away, feeling, as my lady readers will very naturally suppose, in not the most amiable humor in the world. I had just got the child, who was pretty hungry, seated in his high chair, when my husband and his guest made their appearance; and I was introduced.

Sorry am I to chronicle the fact - but truth compels me to make a faithful record - that my reception of the stranger was by no means gracious. I tried to smile; but a smile was such a mockery of my real feelings, that every facial muscle refused to play the hypocrite. The man was not welcome, and it was impossible for me to conceal this.

"A plain family dinner, you see," said Mr. Smith, as we took our places at the meagre board. "We are plain people. Shall I help you to some of the ham and eggs?"

He tried to smile pleasantly, and to seem very much at his ease. But, the attempt was far from successful.

"I want some! Don't give him all!" screamed out the hungry child at my side, stretching out his hands towards the poorly supplied dish, from which my husband was about supplying our guest.

My face, which was red enough before, now became like scarlet. A moment longer I remained at the table, and then rising up quickly took the impatient child in my arms, and carried him screaming from the room. I did not return to grace the dinner table with my unattractive presence. Of what passed, particularly, between my husband and his friend Mr. Jones, who had left his luxurious dinner at the hotel to enjoy "a plain family dinner" with his old acquaintance, I never ventured to make enquiry. They did not remain very long at the table; nor very long in the house after finishing their frugal meal.

T. S. Arthur

I have heard since that Mr. Jones has expressed commiseration for my husband, as the married partner of a real termigant. I don't much wonder at his indifferent opinion; for, I rather think I must have shown in my face something of the indignant fire that was in me.

Mr. Smith, who was too much in the habit of inviting people home to take a "family dinner" with him on the spur of the moment, has never committed that error since. His mortification was too severe to be easily forgotten.

CHAPTER VIII

WHO IS KRISS KRINGLE?

IT was the day before Christmas - always a day of restless, hopeful excitement among the children; and my thoughts were busy, as is usual at this season, with little plans for increasing the gladness of my happy household. The name of the good genius who presides over toys and sugar plums was often on my lips, but oftener on the lips of the children.

"Who is Kriss Kringle, mamma?" asked a pair of rosy lips, close to my ear, as I stood at the kitchen table, rolling out and cutting cakes.

I turned at the question, and met the earnest gaze of a couple of bright eyes, the roguish owner of which had climbed into a chair for the purpose of taking note of my doings.

I kissed the sweet lips, but did not answer.

"Say, mamma? Who is Kriss Kringle?" persevered the little one.

"Why, don't you know?" said I, smiling.

"No, mamma. Who is he?"

"Why, he is - he is - Kriss Kringle."

T. S. Arthur

"Oh, mamma! Say, won't you tell me?"

"Ask papa when. he comes home," I returned, evasively.

I never like deceiving children in any thing. And yet, Christmas after Christmas, I have imposed on them the pleasant fiction of Kriss Kringle, without suffering very severe pangs of conscience. Dear little creatures! how fully they believed, at first, the story; how soberly and confidingly they hung their stockings in the chimney corner; with what faith and joy did they receive their many gifts on the never-to-be-forgotten Christmas morning!

Yes, it is a pleasant fiction; and if there be in it a leaven of wrong, it is indeed a small portion.

"But why won't you tell me, mamma?" persisted my little interrogator. "Don't you know Kriss Kringle?"

"I never saw him, dear," said I.

"Has papa seen him?"

"Ask him when he comes home."

"I wish Krissy would bring me, Oh, such an elegant carriage and four horses, with a driver that could get down and go up again."

"If I see him, I'll tell him to bring you just such a nice carriage."

"And will he do it, mamma?" The dear child clapped his hands together with delight.

"I guess so."

"I wish I could see him," he said, more soberly and thoughtfully.

And then, as if some new impression had crossed his mind, he hastened down from the chair, and went gliding from the room.

Half an hour afterwards, as I came into the nursery, I saw my three "olive branches," clustered together in a corner, holding grave counsel on some subject of importance; at least to themselves. They became silent at my presence; but soon began to talk aloud. I listened to a few words, but perceived nothing of particular concern; then turned my thoughts away.

"Who is Kriss Kringle, papa?" I heard my cherry-lipped boy asking of Mr. Smith, soon after he came home in the evening.

The answer I did not hear. Enough that the enquirer did not appear satisfied therewith.

At tea-time, the children were not in very good appetite, though in fine spirits.

As soon as the evening meal was over, Mr. Smith went out to buy presents for our little ones, while I took upon myself the task of getting them off early to bed.

A Christmas tree had been obtained during the day, and it stood in one of the parlors, on a table. Into this parlor the good genius was to descend during the night, and hang on the branches of the tree, or leave upon the table, his gifts for the children. This was our arrangement. The little ones expressed some doubts as to whether Kriss Kringle would come to this particular room; and little "cherry lips" couldn't just see how the genius was going to get down the chimney, when the fireplace was closed up.

"Never mind, love; Kriss will find his way here," was my answer to all objections.

"But how do you know, mother? Have you sent him word?"

"Oh, I know."

Thus I put aside their enquiries, and hurried them off to bed.

"Now go to sleep right quickly," said I, after they were snugly under their warm blankets and comforts; "and to-morrow morning be up bright and early."

And so I left them to their peaceful slumbers.

An hour it was, or more, ere Mr. Smith returned, with his pockets well laden. I was in the parlor, where we had placed the Christmas tree, engaged in decorating it with rosettes, sugar toys, and the like. At this work I had been some fifteen or twenty minutes, and had, I will own, become a little nervous. My domestic had gone out, and I was alone in the house. Once or twice, as I sat in the silent room, I imagined that I heard a movement in the one adjoining. And several times I was sure that my ear detected something like the smothered breathing of a man.

"All imagination," said I to myself. But again and again the same sounds stirred upon the silent air.

"Could there be a robber concealed in the next room?"

The thought made me shudder. I was afraid to move from where I sat. What a relief when I heard my husband's key in the door, followed by the sound of his well known tread in the passage! My fears vanished in a moment.

As Mr. Smith stood near me, in the act of unloading his pockets, he bent close to my ear and whispered:

"Will is under the table. I caught a glance. of his bright eyes, just now."

"What!"

"It's true. And the other little rogues are in the next room, peeping through the door, at this very moment."

I was silent with surprise.

"They're determined to know who Kriss Kringle is," added my husband; then speaking aloud, he said:

"Come, dear, I want to show you something up in the dining-room."

I understood Mr. Smith, and arose up instantly, not so much as glancing towards the partly opened folding door.

We were hardly in the dining room before we heard the light pattering of feet, and low, smothered tittering on the stairway. Then all was still, and we descended to the parlors again, quite as much pleased with what had occurred as the little rogues were themselves.

"I declare! Really, I thought them all sound asleep an hour ago," said I, on resuming my work of decorating the Christmas tree, "Who could have believed them cunning enough for this? It's all Will's doings. He'll get through the world."

"Aye will he," returned Mr. Smith. "Oh if you could have seen his face as I saw it, just peering from under the table cloth, his eyes as bright as stars, and full of merriment and delight."

"Bless his heart! He's a dear little fellow!"

How could I help saying this?

"And the others! You lost half the pleasure of the whole affair by not seeing them."

"We shall have a frolic with the rogues to-morrow morning. I can see the triumph on Will's face. I understand now what all their whisperings meant this afternoon. They were concocting

T. S. Arthur

this plan. I couldn't have believed it of them?"

"Children are curious bodies," said Mr. Smith.

"I thought I heard some one in the next room," I remarked, "while you were out, and became really nervous for a while. I heard the breathing of some one near me, also; but tried to argue myself into the belief that it was only imagination."

Thus we conned over the little incident, while we arranged the children's toys.

"I know who Kriss Kringle is! I know!" was the triumphant affirmation of one and another of the children, as we gathered at the breakfast table next morning.

"Do you, indeed?" said I, trying to look grave.

"Yes; it is papa."

"Papa, Kriss Kringle! How can that be?"

"Oh, we know! We found out!"

"Indeed!"

And we, made, of course, a great wonder of this assertion. The merry elves! What a happy Christmas it was for them. Ever since, they have dated from the time when they found out who Kriss Kringle was. It is all to no purpose that we pleasantly suggest the possibility of their having dreamed of what they allege to have occurred under their actual vision; they have recorded it in their memories, and refer to it as a veritable fact.

Dear children! How little they really ask of us, to make them happy. Did we give them but a twentieth part of the time we devote to business, care, and pleasure, how greatly would we promote their good, and increase the measure of their enjoyment. Not alone at Christmas time, but all the year should we remember and care for their pleasures; for, the state of innocent pleasure, in children, is one in which good affections are implanted, and these take root and grow, and produce fruit in after life.

T. S. Arthur

CHAPTER IX

NOT AT HOME

NEVER but once did I venture upon the utterance of that little white lie, "Not at home," and then I was well punished for my weakness and folly. It occurred at a time when there were in my family two new inmates: a niece from New York, and a raw Irish girl that I had taken a few days before, on trial.

My niece, Agnes, was a young lady in her nineteenth year, the daughter of my brother. I had not seen her before since her school-girl days; and knew little of her character. Her mother I had always esteemed as a right-thinking, true-hearted woman. I was much pleased to have a visit from Agnes, and felt drawn toward her more and more every day. There was something pure and good about her.

"Now, Aggy, dear," said I to her, one morning after breakfast, as we took our work and retired from the dining-room to one of the parlors, where I was occasionally in the habit of sitting, - "we must sew for dear life until dinner time, so as to finish these two frocks for the children to wear this evening. It isn't right, I know, to impose on you in this way. But you sew so quick and neatly; and then it will help me through, and leave me free to visit Girard College with you this afternoon."

"Don't speak of it, aunt," returned Agnes. - "I'm never happier than when employed. And, besides, it's only fair that I should sew for you in the morning, if you are to go pleasuring with me in the afternoon."

Lightly the hours flew by, passed in cheerful conversation. I found that the mind of my niece had been highly cultivated; that her tastes were refined, and her moral sense acute. To say that I was pleased with her, would but half express what I felt.

There was to be a juvenile party at the house of one of our acquaintances that evening, to which the children were invited; and we were at work in preparing dresses and other matters suitable for them to appear in.

Twelve o'clock came very quickly - too quickly for me, in fact; for I had not accomplished near so much as I had hoped to do. It would require the most diligent application, through every moment of time that intervened until the dinner hour, for us to get through with what we were doing, so as to have the afternoon to ourselves for the intended excursion.

As the clock rung out the hour of noon, I exclaimed:

"Is it possible! I had no idea that it was so late. How slowly I do seem to get along!"

Just at this moment the bell rung.

"Bless me! I hope we are not to have visitors this morning," said I, as I let my hands fall in my lap. I thought hurriedly for a moment, and then remarked, in a decided way:

"Of course we cannot see any one. We are engaged."

By this time I heard the footsteps of Mary on her way from the kitchen, and I very naturally passed quickly to the parlor door to intercept and give her my instructions.

"Say that I'm engaged," was on my tongue. But, somehow or other, I had not the courage to give these words utterance. The visitor might be a person to whom such an excuse for not

T. S. Arthur

appearing would seem unkind, or be an offence. In this uncertain state, my mind fell into confusion. Mary was before me, and awaiting the direction she saw that I was about giving.

"Say that I'm not at home, if any one asks to see me," came in a sudden impulse from my lips.

And then my cheeks flushed to think that I had instructed my servant to give utterance to a falsehood.

"Yes, mim," answered the girl, glancing into my face with a knowing leer, that produced an instant sense of humiliation; and away she went to do my bidding.

I did not glance towards Agnes, as I returned to my seat and took up my work. I had not the courage to do this. That I had lowered myself in her estimation, I felt certain. I heard the street door open, and bent, involuntarily, in a listening attitude. The voice of a lady uttered my name.

"She's not at home, mim," came distinctly on my ears, causing the flush on my cheeks to become still deeper.

A murmur of voices followed. Then I heard the closing of the vestibule door, and Mary returning to the back parlor where we were sitting.

"Who was it, Mary?" I enquired, as the girl entered.

"Mrs. - Mrs. - Now what was it? Sure, and I've forgotten their names intirely."

But, lack of memory did not long keep me in ignorance as to who were my visitors, for, as ill luck would have it, they had bethought themselves of some message they wished to leave, and, re-opening the vestibule door, left a-jar by Mary, followed her along the passage to the room they saw her enter. As they pushed open the door of the parlor, Mary heard them, and, turning quickly, exclaimed, in consternation -

"Och, murther!"

A moment she stood, confronting, in no very graceful attitude, a couple of ladies, and then escaped to the kitchen.

Here was a scene of embarrassment. Not among all my acquaintances were there, perhaps, two persons, whom I would have least desired to witness in me such a fault as the one of which I had been guilty. For a little while, I knew not what to say. I sat, overcome with mortification. At length, I arose, and said with an effort,

"Walk in, ladies! How are you this morning? I'm pleased to see you. Take chairs. My niece, Mrs. Williams, and Mrs. Glenn. I hope you will excuse us. We were - "

"Oh, no apologies, Mrs. Smith," returned one of the ladies, with a quiet smile, and an air of self-possession. "Pardon this intrusion. We understood the servant that you were not at home."

"Engaged, she meant," said I, a deeper crimson suffusing my face. "The fact is, we are working for dear life, to get the children ready for a party to-night, and wished to be excused from seeing any one."

"Certainly - all right," returned Mrs. Williams, "I merely came in to say to your domestic (I had forgotten it at the door) that my sister expected to leave for her home in New York in a day or two, and would call here with me, to-morrow afternoon."

"I shall be very happy to see her," said I, - "very happy. Do come in and sit down for a little while. If I had only known it was you."

Now that last sentence, spoken in embarrassment and mental confusion, was only making matters worse. It placed me in a false and despicable light before my visitors; for in it was the savor of hypocrisy, which is foreign to my nature.

T. S. Arthur

"No, thank you," replied my visitors. "Good morning!"

And they retired, leaving me so overcome with shame, mortification, confusion, and distress, that I burst into tears.

"To think that I should have done such a thing!" was my first remark, so soon as I had a little recovered my self-possession; and I looked up, half timidly, into the face of my niece. I shall not soon forget the expression of surprise and pain that was in her fair young countenance. I had uttered a falsehood in her presence, and thus done violence to the good opinion she had formed of me. The beautiful ideal of her aunt, which had filled her mind, was blurred over; and her heart was sad in consequence.

"Dear Aggy!" said I, throwing my work upon the floor, and bending earnestly towards her. - "Don't think too meanly of me for this little circumstance. I never was guilty of that thing before - never! And well have I been punished for my thoughtless folly I spoke from impulse, and not reflection, when I told Mary to say that I was not at home, and repented of what I had done almost as soon as the words passed my lips."

Agnes looked at me for some moments, until her eyes filled with tears. Then she said in a low, sweet, earnest voice:

"Mother always says, if she cannot see any one who calls, that she is engaged."

"And so do I, dear," I returned. "This is my first offence against truth, and you may be sure that it will be the last."

And it was my last.

When next I met Mrs. Williams and Mrs. Glenn, there was, in both of them, a reserve not seen before. I felt this change keenly. I had wronged myself in their good opinion; and could not venture upon an explanation of my conduct; for that, I felt, might only make matters worse.

How often, since, has my cheek burned, as a vivid recollection came up before my mind of what occurred on that morning! I can never forget it.

T. S. Arthur

CHAPTER X

SHIRT BUTTONS

IN a previous chapter, I gave the reader one of the Experiences of my sister's husband, Mr. John Jones. I now give another.

There was a time in my married life, (thus Mr. Jones writes, in one of *his* "Confessions,") when I was less annoyed if my bosom or wristband happened to be minus a button, than I am at present. But continual dropping will wear away a stone, and the ever recurring buttonless collar or wristband will wear out a man's patience, be he naturally as enduring as the Man Of Uz.

I don't mean by this, that Mrs. Jones is a neglectful woman. Oh, no! don't let that be imagined for a moment. Mrs. Jones is a woman who has an eye for shirt buttons, and when that is said, a volume is told in a few words.

But I don't care how careful a wife is, nor how good an eye she may have for shirt buttons, there will come a time, when, from some cause or other, she will momentarily abate her vigilance, and that will be the very time when Betty's washing-board, or Nancy's sad-iron, has been at work upon the buttons.

For a year or two after our marriage, I used to express impatience, whenever, in putting on a clean shirt, I found a button gone. Mrs. Jones, bore this for a while without exhibiting much feeling. But it fretted her more than she permitted any one to see. At length, the constant recurrence of the evil - I didn't know as much then as I do now - annoyed me so that I passed from ejaculatory expressions of impatience into more decided and emphatic disapprobation, and to

"Psha!" and "there it is again!" and the like were added:

"I declare, Mrs. Jones, this is too bad!" or

"I've given up hoping for a shirt with a full complement of buttons - " or

"If you can't sew the buttons on my shirt, Mrs. Jones, I will hire some one to do it."

This last expression of displeasure I never ventured upon but once. I have always felt ashamed of it since, whenever a recollection of my unreasonableness and impatience in the early times of the shirt button trouble has crossed my mind. My wife took it so much to heart, and so earnestly avowed her constant solicitude in regard to the shirt buttons, that I resolved from that time, to bear the evil like a man, and instead of grumbling or complaining, make known the fact of a deficiency whenever it occurred, as a good joke. And so for a year or so it used to be when the buttons were missing:

"Buttons again, Mrs. Jones;" or

"D'ye see that?" or

"Here's the old story" -

Always said laughingly, and varied as to the mood or fertility of fancy. But on so grave a subject as shirt buttons, Mrs. Jones had no heart for a joke. The fact that her vigilance had proved all in vain, and that, spite of constant care, a shirt had found its way into my drawer, lacking its full complement of buttons, was something too serious for a smile or a jest, and my words, no matter how lightly spoken, would be felt as a reproof. Any allusion, therefore, to shirt buttons, was sure to produce a

T. S. Arthur

cloud upon the otherwise calm brow of Mrs. Jones. It was a sore subject, and could not be touched even by the light end of a feather without producing pain.

What was I to do? Put off with the lack of a shirt button uncomplainingly? Pin my collar, if the little circular piece of bone or ivory were gone, and not hint at the omission? Yes; I resolved not to say a word more about shirt buttons, but to bear the evil, whenever it occurred, with the patience of a martyr. Many days had not passed after this resolution was taken, before, on changing my linen one morning, I found that there was a button less than the usual number on the bosom of my shirt. Mrs. Jones had been up on the evening before, half an hour after I was in bed, looking over my shirts, to see if every thing was in order. But even her sharp eyes had failed to discover the place left vacant by a deserting member of the shirt button fraternity. I knew she had done her best, and I pitied, rather than blamed her, for I was sensible that a knowledge of the fact which had just come to light would trouble her a thousand times more than it did me.

The breakfast hour passed without a discovery by Mrs. Jones of the fact that there was a button off of the bosom of my shirt. But, when I came in at dinner time, her first words, looking at me, were: "Why, Mr. Jones, there's a button off your bosom."

"I know," said I, indifferently. "It was off when I put the shirt on this morning. But it makes no difference - you can sew it on when the shirt next comes from the wash."

I was really sincere in what I said, and took some merit to myself for being as composed as I was on so agitating subject. Judge of my surprise, then, to hear Mrs. Jones exclaim, with a flushed face, "Indeed, Mr. Jones, this is too much! no difference, indeed? A nice opinion people must have had of your wife, to see you going about with your bosom all gaping open in that style?"

"Nobody noticed it," said I in reply. "Don't you see that the edges lie perfectly smooth together, as much so as if held by a button?"

But it was no use to say anything; Mrs. Jones was hurt at my not speaking of the button.

"I'm sure," she said, "that I am always ready to do anything for you. I never complain about sewing on your buttons."

"Nonsense, Mrs. Jones! don't take it so much to heart," I replied; "here, get your needle and thread, and you can have it all right in a minute. It's but a trifle - I'm sure I havn't thought about it since I put on the shirt this morning."

But all would not do - Mrs. Jones' grief was too real; and when I, losing to some extent, my patience, said fretfully, "I wish somebody would invent a shirt without buttons," she sighed deeply, and in a little while I saw her handkerchief go quietly to her eyes. Again and again I tried the say-nothing plane; but it worked worse, if any thing, than the other; for Mrs. Jones was sure to find out the truth, and then she would be dreadfully hurt about my omission to speak.

And so the years have passed. Sometimes I fret a little when I find a shirt button off; sometimes I ask mildly to have the omission supplied when I discover its existence; sometimes I jest about it, and sometimes I bear the evil in silence. But the effects produced upon Mrs. Jones are about the same. Her equanimity of mind is disturbed, and she will look unhappy for hours. Never but once have I complained without a cause. But that one instance gave Mrs. Jones a triumph which has done much to sustain her in all her subsequent trials.

We had some friends staying with us, and among the various matters of discussion that came up during the social evenings we spent together, shirt buttons were, on one occasion, conspicuous. To record all that was said about them would fill pages, and I will not, therefore, attempt even a brief record of

T. S. Arthur

all the allegations brought against the useful little shirt button. The final decision was, that it must be the Apple of Discord in disguise.

"A button off, as usual!" I muttered to myself the next morning, as I put on a clean shirt. Mrs. Jones had risen half an hour before me, and was down stairs giving some directions about breakfast, so that I could not ask to have it sewed on.

And after leaving my room, I thought it as well not to say any thing about it. In due time we gathered with our friends around the breakfast table. A sight of them reminded me of the conversation the previous evening, and I felt an irresistible desire to allude to the missing shirt button as quite an apropos and amusing incident. So, speaking from the impulse of the moment, I said, glancing first at Mrs. Jones, then around the table, and then pointing down at my bosom, "The old story of shirt buttons again!"

Instantly the color mounted to the cheeks and brow of Mrs. Jones; then the color as quickly melted away, and a look of triumph passed over her face. She pushed back her chair quickly, and rising up, came round to where I sat, took hold of the button I had failed to see, and holding it between her fingers, said, "Oh, yes, this *is* the old story, Mr. Jones!"

I drew down my chin so as to get a low angle of vision, and sure enough, the button was there. A burst of laughter went around the table, in which Mrs. Jones most heartily joined; and I laughed, too, as glad as she was, that the joke was all on her side. I have never, you may be sure, heard the last of this; but it was a lucky incident, for it has given Mrs. Jones something to fall back upon, and have her jest occasionally, whenever I happen to discover that a button is among the missing, and that she can, even at times, find it in her heart to jest on such a subject, is, I can assure you, a great gain. So much for shirt buttons. I could say a great deal more, for the subject is inexhaustible. But I will forbear.

CHAPTER XI

PAVEMENT WASHING IN WINTER

TWO weeks of spring-like weather in mid-winter, and then the thermometer went hurrying down towards zero with alarming rapidity. Evening closed in with a temperature so mild that fires were permitted to expire in the ashes; and morning broke with a cold nor-wester, whistling through every crack and cranny, in a tone that made you shrink and shiver.

"Winter at last," said I, creeping forth from my warm bed, with a very natural feeling of reluctance.

"Time," was the half asleep and half awake response of Mr. Smith, as he drew the clothes about his shoulders, and turned himself over for the enjoyment of his usual half hour morning nap.

It was Saturday - that busiest day in the seven; at least for housekeepers - and as late as half past seven o'clock, yet the house felt as cold as a barn. I stepped to the register to ascertain if the fire had been made in the heater. Against my hand came a pressure of air - cold air.

"Too bad!" I murmured fretfully, "that girl has never touched the fire."

So I gave the bell a pretty vigorous jerk. In a few minutes up came Nancy, the cook, in answer to my summons.

T. S. Arthur

"Why hasn't Biddy made the fire in the heater?" I asked.

"She has made it, mum."

"There isn't a particle of heat coming up."

"I heard her at work down there. I guess she's made it up, but it hasn't began to burn good yet."

"Tell her that I want her."

"She's washing the pavement, mum."

"Washing the pavement!"

"Yes, mum."

"What possessed her to wash the pavement on a day like this?"

"It's the right day, mum. It's Saturday."

"Saturday! Don't she know that the water will freeze almost as soon as it touches the ground? Go and tell her to come in this minute, and not throw another drop on the pavement."

Nancy withdrew, and I kept on speaking to myself -

"I never saw such creatures. No consideration in them! Washing the pavement on a morning like this! Little do they care who falls on the ice; or who has a broken arm, or a broken leg."

Just as I had said this, I heard a crash, and an exclamation without, and hurrying to the window looked forth. Biddy's work was done, and well done, for the pavement was one sheet of ice, as hard and smooth as glass, and as slippery as oil. Prostrate thereon was a grocer's boy, and just beyond the curb stone, in the gutter, lay the fragments of a jug of molasses.

Stepping back quickly to where the bell rope hung against the wall, I gave it a most determined jerk. Scarcely had I done this, ere the door of the adjoining room, which was used as a nursery, opened, and Biddy appeared therein.

"Why, Biddy!" I exclaimed, "what possessed you to throw water on the pavement this morning?"

"Faix! And how was I to get it clane, mim, widout wather?" coolly returned Biddy.

"Clean!"

"Yes, mim, clane."

"There was no crying necessity to have it clean to-day. Didn't you see - "

"It's Sathurday, mim," interrupted Biddy, in a voice that showed the argument in her mind to be unanswerable. "We always wash the pavement on Sathurday."

"But it doesn't do to wash the pavement," I returned, now trying to put a little reason into her head, "when it is so cold that water will freeze as soon as it touches the ground. The bricks become as slippery as glass, and people can't walk on them without falling."

"Och! And what hev we till do wid the paple. Lot 'em look 'till their steps."

"But, Biddy, that won't do. People don't expect to find pavements like glass; and they slip, often, while unaware of danger. Just at this moment a poor lad fell, and broke his jug all to pieces."

"Did he! And less the pity for him. Why did'nt he walk along like an orderly, dacent body? Why didn't he look 'till his steps?"

T. S. Arthur

"Biddy," said I, seeing that it was useless to hold an argument with her, - "Do you go this minute and throw ashes all over the pavement."

"Ashes on the clane pavement! Mrs. Smith!"

"Yes, Biddy; and do it at once. There! Somebody else has fallen."

I sprung to the window in time to see a woman on the pavement, and the contents of her basket of marketing scattered all around her.

"Go this minute and throw ashes over the pavement!" I called to Biddy in a voice of command.

The girl left the room with evident reluctance. The idea of scattering ashes over her clean pavement, was, to her, no very pleasant one.

It seemed to me, as I sat looking down from my windows upon the slippery flags, and noted the difficulty which pedestrians had to cross them safely, that Biddy would never appear with her pan of ashes.

"Why don't the girl do as I directed?" had just passed, in an impatient tone, from my lips, when two well dressed men came in view, one at each (sic) exteremtiy of the sheet of ice. They were approaching, and stepped with evident unconscio- usness of danger, upon the treacherous surface. I had a kind of presentiment that one or both would fall, and my instinct was not at fault. Suddenly the heels of one flew up, and he struck the pavement with a concussion that sprung his hat from his head, and sent it some feet in the air. In his efforts to recover himself, his legs became entangled in those of the other, and over he went, backwards, his head striking the ground with a terrible shock.

I started from the window, feeling, for an instant, faint and sick. In a few moments I returned, and looked out again. Both the fallen ones had regained their feet, and passed out of sight, and Biddy, who had witnessed the last scene in this half comic, half tragic performance, was giving the pavement a plentiful coating of ashes and cinders.

I may be permitted to remark, that I trust other housekeepers, whose pavements are washed on cold mornings - and their name, I had almost said, is legion - are as innocent as I was in the above case, and that the wrong to pedestrians lies at the door of thoughtless servants. But is it not our duty to see the wrong has no further repetition?

It has been remarked that the residence of a truly humane man may be known by the ashes before his door on a slippery morning. If this be so, what are we to think of those who coolly supply a sheet of ice to the side walk?

T. S. Arthur

CHAPTER XII

REGARD FOR THE POOR

WE sometimes get, by chance, as it were, glimpses of life altogether new, yet full of instruction. I once had such a glimpse, and, at the time, put it upon record as a lesson for myself as well as others. Its introduction into this series of "Confessions" will be quite in place.

"How many children have you?" I asked of a poor woman, one day, who, with her tray of fish on her head, stopped at my door with the hope of finding a customer.

"Four," she replied.

"All young?"

"Yes ma'am. The oldest is but seven years of age."

"Have you a husband?" I enquired.

The woman replied in a changed voice:

"Yes, ma'am. But he isn't much help to me. Like a great many other men, he drinks too much. If it wasn't for that, you wouldn't find me crying fish about the streets in the spring, and berries through the summer, to get bread for my children. He could support us all comfortably, if he was only sober; for he has a good trade, and is a good workman. He used to earn ten and sometimes twelve dollars a week."

"How much do you make towards supporting your family?" I asked.

"Nearly all they get to live on, and that isn't much," she said bitterly. "My husband sometimes pays the rent, and sometimes he doesn't even do that. I have made as high as four dollars in a week, but oftener two or three is the most I get."

"How in the world can you support yourself, husband, and four children on three dollars a week?"

"I have to do it," was her simple reply. "There are women who would be glad to get three dollars a week, and think themselves well off."

"But how do you live on so small a sum?"

"We have to deny ourselves almost every little comfort, and confine ourselves down to the mere necessaries of life. After those who can afford to pay good prices for their marketing have been supplied, we come in for a part of what remains. I often get meat enough for a few cents to last me for several days. And its the same way with vegetables. After the markets are over, the butchers and country people, whom we know, let us have lots of things for almost nothing, sooner than take them home. In this way we make our slender means go a great deal farther than they would if we had to pay the highest market price for every thing. But, it often happens that what we gain here is lost in the eagerness we feel to sell whatever we have, especially when, from having walked and cried for a long time, we become much fatigued. Almost every one complains that we ask too much for our things, if we happen to be one or two cents above what somebody has paid in market, where there are almost as many different prices as there are persons who sell. And in consequence, almost every one tries to beat us down.

T. S. Arthur

"It often happens that, after I have walked for hours and sold but very little, I have parted with my whole stock at cost to some two or three ladies, who would not have bought from me at all if they hadn't known that they were making good bargains out of me; and this because I could not bear up any longer. I think it very hard, sometimes, when ladies, who have every thing in plenty, take off nearly all my profits, after I have toiled through the hot sun for hours, or shivered in the cold of winter. It is no doubt right enough for every one to be prudent, and buy things as low as possible; but it has never seemed to me as quite just for a rich lady to beat down a poor fish-woman, or strawberry-woman, a cent or two on a bunch or basket, when that very cent made, perhaps, one-third, or one-half of her profits.

"It was only yesterday that I stopped at a house to sell a bunch of fish. The lady took a fancy to a nice bunch of small rock, for which I asked her twenty cents. They had cost me just sixteen cents. 'Won't you take three fips?' she asked. 'That leaves me too small a profit, madam,' I replied. 'You want too much profit,' she returned; 'I saw just such a bunch of fish in market yesterday for three fips.' 'Yes, but remember,' I replied, 'that here are the fish at your door. You neither have to send for them nor to bring them home yourself.' 'Oh, as to that,' she answered, 'I have a waiter whose business it is to carry the marketing. It is all the same to me. So, if you expect to sell me your things, you must do it at the market prices. I will give you three fips for that bunch of fish, and no more.' I had walked a great deal, and sold but little. I was tired, and half sick with a dreadful headache. It was time for me to think about getting home. So I said, 'Well, ma'am, I suppose you must take them, but it leaves me only a mere trifle for my profit.' A servant standing by took the fish, and the lady handed me a quarter, and held out her hand for the change. I first put into it a five cent piece. She continued holding it out, until I searched about in ny pocket for a penny. This I next placed in her hand. 'So you've cheated me out of a cent at last,' she said, half laughing and half in earnest; 'you are a sad rogue.' A little boy was standing by. 'Here, Charley,' she said to him, 'is a penny I have just saved. You can buy a candy with it.'

"As I turned away from the door of the large, beautiful house in which that lady lived, I felt something rising in my throat and choking me; I had bitter thoughts of all my kind.

"Happily, where I next stopped, I met with one more considerate. She bought two bunches of my fish at my own price - spoke very kindly, to me, and even went so far, seeing that I looked jaded out, to tell me to go down into her kitchen and rest myself for a little while.

"Leaving my tub of fish in her yard, I accepted the kind offer. It so happened that the cook was making tea for some one in the house who was sick. The lady asked me if I would not like to have a cup. I said yes; for my head was aching badly, and I felt faint; and besides, I had not tasted a cup of tea for several days. She poured it out with her own hands, and with her own hands brought it to me. I think I never tasted such a cup of tea in my life. It was like cordial. God bless her! - When I again went out upon the street my headache was gone, and I felt as fresh as ever I did in my life. Before I stopped at this kind lady's house, I was so worn down and out of heart, that I determined to go home, even though not more than half my fish were sold. But now I went on cheerful and with confidence. In an hour my tray was empty, and my fish sold at fair prices.

"You do not know, madam," continued the woman, "how much good a few kindly spoken words, that cost nothing, or a little generous regard for us, does our often discouraged hearts. But these we too rarely meet. Much oftener we are talked to harshly about our exorbitant prices - called a cheating set - or some such name that does not sound very pleasant to our ears. That there are many among us who have no honesty, nor, indeed, any care about what is right, is too true. But all are not so. To judge us all, then, by the worst of our class, is not right. It would not be well for the world if all were thus judged."

T. S. Arthur

CHAPTER XIII

SOMETHING MORE ABOUT COOKS

FOR sometime I had a treasure of a cook; a fine Bucks county girl, whose strongest recommendation in my eyes, when I engaged her, was that she had never been out of sight of land. But she left my house for a "better place," as she said. I might have bribed her to remain, by an offer of higher wages; but, experience had demonstrated to my satisfaction, that this kind of bribery never turns out well. Your servant, in most instances, soon becomes your mistress - or, at least, makes bold efforts to assume that position.

So, I let my Bucks county girl go to her "better place." As to how or why it was to be a better place, I did not make enquiry. That was her business. She was a free agent, and I did not attempt to influence her. In fact, being of rather an independent turn of mind myself, I sympathize with others in their independence, and rarely seek to interfere with a declared course of action.

My new cook, unfortunately, had been out of sight of land, and that for weeks together. She was fresh from the Emerald Island. When she presented herself I saw in her but small promise. Having learned on enquiry that her name was Alice Mahoney, I said:

"How long have you been in this country, Alice?"

There was a moment or two of hesitation. Then she answered:

"Sax months, mum."

I learned afterwards that she had arrived only three days before.

"Can you cook?" I enquired.

"Och, yis! Ony thing, from a rib of bafe down till a parate."

"You're sure of that, Alice?"

"Och! sure, mum."

"Can you give me a reference?"

"I've got a character from Mrs. Jordan, where I lived in New York. I've only been here a few days. Biddy Jones knows me."

And she produced a written testification of ability, signed "Mary Jones, No. - William street, New York." There was a suspicious look about this "character;" but of course I had no means of deciding whether it were a true or false document.

After some debate with myself, I finally decided to give Alice a trial.

It so happened that on the very day she came, an old lady friend of my mother's, accompanied by her two daughters, both married and housekeepers, called to spend the afternoon and take tea. As they lived at some distance, I had tea quite early, not waiting for Mr. Smith, whose business kept him away pretty late.

During the afternoon, my "butter man" came. Occasionally he brings some very nice country sausages, and I always make it a point to secure a few pounds when he does so. He had some on this occasion.

T. S. Arthur

"Alice," said I, as I entered the kitchen about four o'clock, "I want you to hurry and get tea ready as quickly as you can."

"Yes, mum," was the ready reply.

"And Alice," I added, "we'll have some of these sausages with the tea. They are very fine ones - better than we usually get. Be sure to cook them very nice."

"Yes, mum," promptly answered the girl, looking quite intelligent.

A few more directions as to what we were to have were given, and then I went up to sit with my company.

It was not my intention to leave all to the doubtful skill of my new cook, but, either the time passed very rapidly, or she was more prompt and active than is usual among cooks, for the tea bell rung before I was in expectation of hearing it.

"Ah," said I, "there is our tea bell," and I arose, adding, "will you walk into the dining-room, ladies?"

The words were no sooner uttered than a doubt as to all being as I could wish crossed my mind; and I regretted that I had not first repaired to the dining-room alone. But, as it was too late now, or, rather, I did not happen to have sufficient presence of mind to recall my invitation to the ladies to walk in to tea, until I had preceded them a few minutes.

Well, we were presently seated at the tea table. My practised eye instantly saw that the cloth was laid crookedly, and that the dishes were placed in a slovenly manner.

I couldn't help a passing apology, on the ground of a new domestic, and then proceeded to the business of pouring out the tea. The cups were handed around, and I soon noticed that my guests were sipping from their spoons in a very unsatisfactory manner. I was in the act of filling my own cup from the tea urn, when I missed the plate of sausages, about which I had boasted to my lady friends as something a little better than were usually to be obtained. So I rung the table bell. Alice presently made her appearance.

"Alice," said I, "where are the sausages I told you to cook? You surely hav'nt forgotten them?"

"Och, no indade, mum. They're there."

"Where? I don't see them."

And my eyes ran around the table.

"They're wid the ta mum, sure!"

"With the tea?"

"Sure, mum, they're wid the ta. Ye towld me yees wanted the sausages wid the ta; and sure they're there. I biled 'em well."

A light now flashed over my mind. Throwing up the lid of the tea urn, I thrust in a fork, which immediately came in contact with a hard substance. I drew it forth, and exhibited a single link of a well "biled" sausage.

Let me draw a veil over what followed.

T. S. Arthur

CHAPTER XIV

NOT A RAG ON THEIR BACKS

THERE are, among the many things which Mr. Smith, like other men, will *not* understand, frequent difficulties about the children's clothing. He seems to think that frocks and trowsers grow spontaneously; or that the dry goods, once bought and brought into the house, will resolve into the shapes desired, and fit themselves to the children's backs, like Cindarella's suit in the nursery tale. Now, I never did claim to be a sprite; and I am not sure that the experience of all housekeepers will bear me out in the opinion that the longer a woman is married, the less she becomes like a fairy.

Stitch! stitch! stitch! Hood's Song of the Shirt, which every body has heard and admired, is certainly most eloquent and pathetic upon the sufferings and difficulties of sewing girls. "Much yet remains unsung," particularly in regard to the ceaseless labors of women who are as rich as Cornelia in muslin-rending, habit-cloth-destroying, children's-plaid-rubbing - jewels! I am sure that the Roman matron never went shopping. I am sure that she did not undertake to keep her own children's clothing in repair; for if she had, she could not have been ready, at a moment's warning, to put forward her troublesome charge as specimen jewels. Do all I can, my little comforts never *are* "fit to be seen!"

Many is the weary evening that I have been occupied, past the noon of night, in repairing the wear and tear of habiliments -

abridging the volume of the elder children's clothes into narrow dimensions for the next, or compiling a suit for one, out of the fringed raiment of two or three. Honest was the pride with which I have surveyed these industrious efforts, and sincere the thought that I had really accomplished something. Depositing the various articles where the wearers elect would find them, I have retired to rest; almost angry with Mr. Smith, who was asleep hours before me - asleep as unconcernedly as if an indestructible substance fabric had been invented for children's clothing.

Well, after such a night's work, imagine me waking, with a complacent and happy sensation that, my work having been *done* on the day before, the morning is open for new employment. Down stairs I come, full of the thoughts of the confusion I shall heap on Mr. Smith's head. He, observe, told me, as he left me to retire, that I had much better go to bed, for all my work would amount to nothing but loss of necessary rest. I am ready to show him triumphant evidence to the contrary, in the clothes, as good as new, in which his children are habited. Before I can speak, I discern a lurking smile in his face. My boy Will stands in a sheepish posture, with his back as close to the jam, as if he were a polypus growing there, and his life depended upon the adhesion.

My eldest girl - another of the laboriously fitted out of the night before, has a marvellous affection for the little stool, and the skirt of her frock seems drawn about her feet in a most unbecoming manner.

But the third, an inveterate little romp, unconscious of shame, is curveting about in the most abandoned manner, utterly indifferent to the fact she has - not, indeed, "a rag to her back" - for she is *all* rags! One hour's play before my descent has utterly abolished all traces of my industry, so far as she is concerned.

I expostulate - at first more in sorrow than in anger - but as Mr. Smith's face expands into a broad laugh, it becomes more anger than sorrow. The child on the stool looks as if she would laugh, if she *dared*. Lifting her up suddenly, I discover that the whole front breadth of her frock is burned - past redemption.

I say nothing - what *can* I say? I have not words equal to the emergency. And the boy - boys *are* such copies of their fathers! He actually forgets all embarrassment, and breaks out into a hearty laugh. I jerk him forward.

Horror on horrors! The unveiling of the Bavarian statue, of which I read an account in the newspapers the other day, is nothing to it. The jamb, it appears, has supported something besides the mantle shelf; for when I draw the young Smith forward, deprived of the friendly aid of the wall, his teguments drop to the floor, and *he* stands unveiled! One fell swoop at rude play has destroyed all my little innumerable stitches; and I am just where I was before I threaded a needle the night before!

Now I appeal to any body - any woman with the least experience, if this is not all *too bad*! And yet my husband insists that I have no need to be continually worrying myself with the needle. It *is* true that each of the children has four or five changes of clothes, which they might wear - but what is the use of their having things to "put right on - and tear right out!" I like to be prudent and saving. It was only the other day that Mr. Smith came in early, and found me busy; and commenced a regular oration. He said that every child in the house has a better wardrobe than he; and so he went on, and counted all off to me. He says - and men think they know *so much* - that if children have clothes they should wear them; and when they are worn out, provide more, and not try to keep as many half-worn suits in repair, as there are new suits in a queen's wardrobe. But he likes, as well as any man, to see his children look neat, whatever he may say. And yet he pretends that children should have clothes so made that they can convert themselves into horses, and treat each other to rides without rending to pieces! And he protests that it is all nonsense to undertake to keep children dressed in the fashion! Truly I am tempted to say to the men as Job did to his friends: "No doubt but ye are the people, and wisdom shall die with you!"

Such plagues as they are sometimes! But I could not help laughing after all, when, as I said before, he was lecturing me. The table was covered with work, done and in progress. He went on till out of breath. I answered:

"Now you know the children have not a rag to their backs!"

"I should think not," he said, drily, as he looked about him. "The other morning finished up the rags on hand - but you are doing your best, with flimsy finery, to get up a new assortment."

"Now, that is unkind in you, Mr. Smith," said I, feeling hurt, and looking and speaking as I felt. "Really unkind in you. I'm sure it's no pleasure for me to work, work, work, from morning till night, until I'm worn down and good for nothing. I wish my children to look decent at least; and to do this at as small cost to you as possible. You can't change me with wasting your property, at least."

"There, there, dear! That will do. Say no more about it," returned Mr. Smith, in a soothing voice. "I didn't mean to be unkind. Still, I do think that you are a little over-particular about the children's clothes, as I have said before - over-particular in the matter of having things *just so*. Better, a great deal, I think, spare a few hours from *extra work* given to the clothing designed for their bodies, to that which is to array and beautify their minds."

"Now, Mr. Smith!" I exclaimed, and then bending my face into my hands, gave way to involuntary tears.

That he should have said this!

T. S. Arthur

CHAPTER XV

CURIOSITY

THE curiosity of our sex is proverbial. Proverbs are generally based upon experience, and this one, I am ready to admit, is not without a good foundation to rest upon.

Our sex are curious; at least I am, and we are very apt to judge others by ourselves. I believe that I have never broken the seal nor peeped into a letter bearing the name of some other lady; but, then, I will own to having, on more occasions than one, felt an exceedingly strong desire to know the contents of certain epistles in the hands of certain of my friends.

The same feeling I have over and over again observed in my domestics, and, for this reason, have always been careful how I let my letters lie temptingly about. One chamber maid in my service, seemed to have a passion for reading other people's letters. More than once had I caught her (sic) rumaging in my drawers, or with some of my old letters in her hands; and I could not help remarking that most of the letters left at the door by the penny post, had, if they passed to me through her, a crumpled appearance. I suspected the cause of this, but did not detect my lady, until she had been some months in my family.

One morning, after breakfast was over, and the children off to school, I drew on a cap, and went down to sweep out and dust the parlors. I had not been at work long, when I heard the bell ring. Presently Mary came tripping down stairs. As she opened the street door, I heard her say:

"Ah! another letter? Who is it for? Me?"

"No, it is for Mrs. Smith," was answered, in the rougher voice of the Despatch Post-man.

"Oh." There was a perceptible disappointment in Mary's tone. "What's the postage?" she asked.

"Paid," said the man.

The door closed, and I heard the feet of Mary slowly moving along the passage. Then the murmur of her voice reached my ears. Presently I heard her say:

"I wonder who it is from? Mrs. Smith gets a great many letters. No envelope, thank goodness! but a plain, good old fashioned letter. I must see who it is from."

By this time Mary had stepped within the back parlor. I stood, hid from her view, by one of the folding doors, which was closed, but within a few feet of her.

"From Mrs. Jackson! Hum - m. I wonder what she's got to say? Something about me, I'll bet a dollar."

There was a very apparent change in the thermometer of Mary's feelings at this last thought, as was evident from the tone of her voice.

"Lace collars - stockings - pocket han - . I can't make out that word, but it is handkerchiefs, of course," thus Mary read and talked to herself. "Breastpin - this is too mean! It's not true, neither. I'm a great mind to burn the letter. Mrs. Smith would never be the wiser. I won't give it to her now, at any rate. I'll put it in my pocket, and just think about it."

T. S. Arthur

The next sound that came to my ears was the pattering of Mary's feet as she went hurrying up the stairs.

In a few minutes I followed. In one of my chambers I found Mary, and said to her:

"Didn't the carrier leave me a letter just now?"

The girl hesitated a moment, and then answered:

"Oh, yes, ma'am. I have it here in my pocket."

And she drew forth the letter, crumbled, as was usually the case with all that passed through her hands.

I took it, with some gravity of manner; for I felt, naturally enough, indignant. Mary flushed a little under the steady eye that I fixed upon her.

The letter, or note, was from my friend, Mrs. Jackman, and read as follows:

> "MY DEAR MRS. SMITH. - Do call in and see me some time to-day. I have bought some of the cheapest laces, stockings, and cambric pocket handkerchiefs that ever were seen. There are more left; and at a great bargain. You must have some. And, by the way, bring with you that sweet breastpin I saw you wear at Mrs. May's last Thursday evening. I want to examine it closely. I must have one just like it. Do come round to-day; I've lots of things to say to you.
>
> Yours, &c."

"Nothing so dreadful in all that," I said to myself, as I re-folded the letter. "My curious lady's conscience must be a little active! Let's see what is to come of this."

It is hardly in the nature of woman to look very lovingly upon the servant whom she has discovered peeping into her letters. At least, it was not in my nature. I, therefore, treated Mary with becoming gravity, whenever we happened to meet. She, under the circumstances, was ill at ease; and rather shunned contact with me. The morning passed away, and the afternoon waned until towards five o'clock, when the accumulating pressure on Mary's feelings became so great that she was compelled to seek relief.

I was alone, sewing, when my chamber maid entered my room. The corners of her lips inclined considerably downward.

"Can I speak a word with you, Mrs. Smith?" said she.

"Certainly, Mary," I replied. "What do you wish to say?"

Mary cleared her throat once or twice - looked very much embarrassed, and at length stammered out.

"You received a letter from Mrs. Jackson this morning?"

"No." I shook my head as I uttered this little monosyllable.

A flush of surprise went over the girl's face.

"Wasn't the letter I gave you from Mrs. Jackson?" she asked.

"No; it was from Mrs. Jackman."

Mary caught her breath, and stammered out, in her confusion:

"Oh, my! I thought it was from Mrs. Jackson. I was sure of it."

"What right had you to think any thing about it?" I asked, with marked severity.

Mary's face was, by this time crimsoned.

I looked at her for some moments, and then, taking from my

T. S. Arthur

drawer Mrs. Jackman's note, handed it to her, and said:

"There's the letter you were so curious about this morning. Read it."

Mary's eyes soon took in the contents. The moment she was satisfied, she uttered a short "Oh!" strongly expressive of mental relief, and handed me back the letter.

"I thought it was from Mrs. Jackson," said the still embarrassed girl, looking confused and distressed.

"You can now retire," said I, "and when another letter is left at my door, be kind enough to consider it my property, not yours. I shall make it my business to see Mrs. Jackson, and ascertain from her why you are so much afraid that she will communicate with me. There's some thing wrong."

Poor Mary still lingered.

"Indeed, Mrs. Smith," she sobbed - "I didn't do nothing wrong at Mrs. Jackson's, but wear her clothes sometimes. Once I just borrowed a breastpin of hers out of her drawer, to wear to a party; and she saw me with it on, and said I had stolen it. But, I'd put my hand in the fire before I'd steal, Mrs. Smith! Indeed, indeed I would. I was only going to wear it to the party; and I didn't think there was any great harm in that."

"Of course there was harm in using other people's things without their consent," I replied, severely. "And I don't wonder that Mrs. Jackson accused you of stealing. But what cause had you for thinking this letter was from Mrs. Jackson?"

"The two names are so near alike, and then Mrs. Jackson speaks about - ."

Here Mary caught herself, and crimsoned still deeper.

"That is," said I, "you took the liberty of peeping into my letter before you gave it to me; and this is not your first offence of the kind."

Mary was too much confounded to speak, or make any effort to excuse herself; and so thought it best to retire.

I called to see Mrs. Jackson that day. She gave Mary a good character, as far as honesty was concerned; but stated plainly her faults, especially her bad habit of wearing her clothes and trinkets, for which offence, in a moment of indignation, she had dismissed her from her service.

I saw no reason to send Mary away. But I gave her a "good talking." I think she is pretty well cured of her propensity of reading other people's letters.

CHAPTER XVI

HOUSE-CLEANING

I LIKE a clean house. So does Mr. Smith, and so do all men, if they would acknowledge it. At any rate, when their dwellings seem a little dingy or dusty - a very thin coat of dinginess or dust over the whole, producing a decidedly bad effect - I say when their dwellings appear to them out of order - though ever so little - *we* are sure to find it out. The dull look of the house appears to be communicated to the countenance of the master thereof. I confess that I have often been half inclined to wax and cork my husband's visage, or at least to whisk over it with the duster, and see if that experiment would not restore its sunny look.

But though men like clean houses, they do not like house-cleaning. They have certain absurd notions which they would wish to carry out; such, for instance, as that constant-quiet, preventive care, or frequent topical applications, carefully applied, would gradually renovate the whole interior. But who wishes to be cleaning all the time? Who wishes to be always dusting? Indeed, at the best, we are constantly with broom, brush, or besom in hand; but the men will not perceive it, and we receive no credit for our tidiness. What is to be done, then? Evidently there is nothing better than a "demonstration," as the politicians say - a demonstration that may be felt; a mass-meeting of brooms, buckets, brushes, paint-pots, white-wash pails, chairs overturned, tubs, coal-skuttles, dust-pans, char-women, and all other possible disagreeables, all at once summoned, and each as much as possible in others' way. In this there is some satisfaction. It looks like *business*. It seems as if you were doing something. It raises the value of the operation, and demonstrates its usefulness and necessity; for if there is little difference apparent between the house before cleaning and after, there is a world of odds between a house-*cleaning* and a house *cleaned*. There is a perfect delight in seeing what order *can* be brought out of chaos, even though you are obliged to make the chaos first, to produce the effect.

I had inflicted several of these impressive lessons upon Mr. Smith. He had become so much horrified at their confusion, that I do believe he had fully reconciled himself to dust and dirt, as the better alternative. They were, to be sure, at some little cost of comfort to myself, and reflectively produced discomfort for him; for he traced, with a correctness which I could easier frown (sic) a than deny, many a week's indisposition to my house-cleaning phrenzy. And when a man's wife is sick, if, he is a man of feeling, he is unhappy. And if he is a man of selfishness, he is wretched, too; for what becomes of husband's little comforts, when wife is not able to procure or direct them? So Mr. Smith, - for the better reason, I believe - pure compassion - declared, long ago, against wholesale house-cleaning. And he has so often interfered in my proceedings with his provoking prophecy, "Now, you know, my dear, it will make you sick," that I have striven many a time to hide pain under a forced smile, when it seemed as if "my head was like to rend."

Now, a woman *can* carry her point in the house by stubborn daring, but "the better part of valor is discretion," and I have learned quietly to take my way, and steal a march upon him; - open the flood-gate - set the chimneys smoking - up with the carpets - throw the beds out of the windows - pack the best china in the middle of the floor distributing pokers and fire-shovels among it - unhang the pictures - set all the doors ajar - roll the children in dust - cover my head with a soiled night-cap - put on slip-shod shoes - and streak my ancles with dust and dirty water. Then, if he pops in opportunely, I can say,

T. S. Arthur

with Shakspeare - amended:

I am in *slops*,

Stept in so far, that, should I wade no more,

Returning were as tedious as go o'er.

And, then, husband has no choice but to retreat to a chop-house, and leave me to finish.

But the chance for a grand saturnalia is best when Mr. Smith goes from home for a day or two. Then I can deny myself to visitors - take full license - set the hydrant running, and puzzle the water commissioners with an extra consumption of Schuylkill. My last exploit in this way was rather disastrous; and I am patiently waiting for its memory to pass away, before I venture even to think of repeating it. Mr. Smith had business in New York – imperative business, he said, - but I do believe it might have waited, had not Jenny Lind's first appearance taken place just then. This by the way. He went, and I was rejoiced to improve the opportunity, for it occurred precisely as I was devising some method to get myself so fairly committed to soap and brushes, that objection or interdict would be too late.

Never did I pack his carpet-bag with more secret satisfaction than on that morning. He was entirely unsuspicious of my intention - though he might have divined it but for having a secret of his own, for Kitty's water-heating operations spoiled the breakfast. There was more than a taste of "overdone" to the steak, and the whole affair, even to me, was intolerable - me, who had the pleasures of house-cleaning in perspective to console me. The door was scarce shut behind him, when I entered into the business *con amore*. It was resolved to begin at the very attic and sweep, scrub, and wash down. Old boxes and trunks were dragged out of their places, and piles of forgotten dust swept out. The passengers in the street had a narrow chance for their beavers and fall bonnets, for every front window had an extra plashing. Mr. Smith had several times urged me to permit him to introduce some Yankee fashion which he highly recommends for having "professional window-cleaners," with their whiting and brushes, who could go through the house with half the trouble, and none of the litter. There's nothing like water.

The first day's work sufficed to put the house into thorough confusion, and I retired to bed - but not to rest, for my fatigue was too great to sleep in comfort. My neglected child rested as ill as myself, - and when I rose the next morning, it was with the oppressive weight of a weary day before me. I had the consciousness that the work *must* be completed before my husband's return; and he had engaged to be with me at dinner. I felt it an imperative duty to welcome him with a cheerful house, and a pleasant repast after his journey; but as the time of his arrival drew near, I was more and more convinced of the impossibility. Like a drove of wild beasts forced into a corner by a hunting party, we forced our unmanageable matters to a crisis. The area for old brooms and brushes, tubs, litter, and slops, was at last narrowed down to the kitchen, and all that remained of our house-cleaning was to put that place into something like the semblance of an apartment devoted to culinary purposes. Dinner, as yet, was unthought of - but the house was clean!

Wearied rather than refreshed by my night of unrest, my arms sore, and my limbs heavy, I labored with double zeal to get up an excitement, which should carry me through the remainder of the day. My head began to feel sensations of giddiness - for I had hardly eaten since my husband left. Of the pleasures of house-cleaning, I had at length a surfeit; when a ring, which I knew among all others, surprised me. I looked at the clock. It was past four, and the kitchen still in confusion, and the hearth cold.

I sank in a chair-in a swoon from sheer exhaustion. When I awoke to consciousness, an overturned pale of water was being absorbed by my clothing, my nose was rejecting with violent aversion the pungency of a bottle of prime Durham mustard, to which Kitty had applied as the best substitute for salts which the kitchen afforded; and my husband, carpet-bag and cane in hand, was pushing his way toward me with more haste than good speed, as the obstacles witnessed, which he encountered and overturned.

I was confined to my room a week - which I could not conceal from Mr. Smith. But he does not even yet know the whole amount of the breakage, and, thank fortune, he is too much of a man to ask. I am only afraid that he will succeed in forcing me to admit, that what he calls his classical proposition is true; that to clean a house does not require the feat of a Hercules, to wit: turning a river through it.

This is my story of house-cleaning, and it is in no very high degree flattering to my housekeeping vanity. Perhaps the thing might be managed differently. But I don't know. Out of chaos, order comes. While on this subject, it will be all in place to introduce another house-cleaning story, which I find floating about in the newspapers. It presents the matter from another point of view, and was written, it will be seen, by a man:

Talk of a washing day! What is that to a whole week of washing-days? No, even this gives no true idea of that worst of domestic afflictions a poor man can suffer - house-cleaning. The washing is confined to the kitchen or wash-house, and the effect visible in the dining-room is in cold or badly cooked meals; with a few other matters not necessary to mention here. But in the house-cleaning - oh, dear! Like the dove from the ark, a man finds no place where he can rest the sole of his foot. Twice a year, regularly, have I to pass through this trying ordeal, *willy-nilly,* as it is said, in some strange language. To rebel is useless. To grumble of no avail. Up come the carpets, topsyturvy goes the furniture, and *swash!* goes the water from garret to cellar. I don't know how other men act on these occasions, but I find discretion the better part of valor, and submission the wisest expedient.

Usually it happens that my good wife works herself half to death - loses the even balance of her mind - and, in consequence, makes herself and all around her unhappy. To indulge in an unamiable temper is by no means a common thing for Mrs. Sunderland, and this makes its occurrence on these occasions so much the harder to bear. Our last house-cleaning took place in the fall. I have been going to write a faithful history of what was said, done, and suffered on the occasion ever since, and now put my design into execution, even at the risk of having my head combed with a three-legged stool by my excellent wife, who, when she sees this in print, will be taken, in nautical phrase, all aback. But, when a history of our own shortcomings, mishaps, mistakes, and misadventures will do others good, I am for giving the history and pocketing the odium, if there be such a thing as odium attached to revelations of human weakness and error.

"We must clean house this week," said my good wife one morning as we sat at the breakfast-table - "every thing is in a dreadful condition. I can't look at nor touch any thing without feeling my flesh creep."

I turned my eyes, involuntarily, around the room. I was not, before, aware of the filthy state in which we were living. But not having so good "an eye for dirt" as Mrs. Sunderland, I was not able, even after having my attention called to the fact, to see "the dreadful condition" of things. I said nothing, however, for I never like to interfere in my wife's department. I assume it as a fact that she knows her own business better than I do.

Our domestic establishment consisted at this time of a cook, chamber maid, and waiter. This was an ample force, my wife considered, for all purposes of house-cleaning, and had so announced to the individuals concerned some days before she mentioned the matter incidentally to me. We had experienced, in common with others, our own troubles with servants, but were now excellently well off in this respect. Things had gone on for months with scarcely a jar.

T. S. Arthur

This was a pleasant feature in affairs, and one upon which we often congratulated ourselves.

When I came home at dinner-time, on the day the anticipated house-cleaning had been mentioned to me, I found my wife with a long face.

"Are you not well?" I asked.

"I'm well enough," Mrs. Sunderland answered, "but I'm out of all patience with Ann and Hannah."

"What is the matter with them?" I asked, in surprise.

"They are both going at the end of this week."

"Indeed! How comes that? I thought they were very well satisfied."

"So they were, all along, until the time for house-cleaning approached. It is too bad!"

"That's it - is it?"

"Yes. And I feel out of all patience about it. It shows such a want of principle."

"Is John going too?" I asked.

"Dear knows! I expect so. He's been as sulky as he could be all the morning - in fact, ever since I told him that he must begin taking up the carpets to-morrow and shake them."

"Do you think Ann and Hannah will really go?" I asked.

"Of course they will. I have received formal notice to supply their places by the end of this week, which I must do, somehow or other."

The next day was Thursday, and, notwithstanding both cook and chamber maid had given notice that they were going on Saturday, my wife had the whole house knocked into *pi*, as the printers say, determined to get all she could out of them.

When I made my appearance at dinner-time, I found all in precious confusion, and my wife heated and worried excessively. Nothing was going on right. She had undertaken to get the dinner, in order that Ann and Hannah might proceed uninterruptedly in the work of house-cleaning; but as Ann and Hannah had given notice to quit in order to escape this very house-cleaning, they were in no humor to put things ahead. In consequence, they had "poked about and done nothing," to use Mrs. Sunderland's own language; at which she was no little incensed.

When evening came, I found things worse. My wife had set her whole force to work upon our chamber, early in the day, in order to have it finished as quickly as possible, that it might be in a sleeping condition by night - dry and well aired. But, instead of this, Ann and Hannah had "dilly-dallied" the whole day over cleaning the paint, and now the floor was not even washed up. My poor wife was a sad way about it; and I am sure that I felt uncomfortable enough. Afraid to sleep in a damp chamber, we put two sofas together in the parlor, and passed the night there.

The morning rose cloudily enough. I understood matters clearly. If Mrs. Sunderland had hired a couple of women for two or three days to do the cleaning, and got a man to shake the carpets, nothing would have been heard about the sulkiness of John, or the notice to quit of cook and chamber maid. Putting upon them the task of house-cleaning was considered an imposition, and they were not disposed to stand it.

"I shall not be home to dinner to-day," I said, as I rose from the breakfast table. "As you are all in so much confusion, and you have to do the cooking, I prefer getting something to eat down town."

"Very well," said Mrs. Sunderland - "so much the better."

I left the house a few minutes afterwards, glad to get away. Every thing was confusion, and every face under a cloud.

"How are you getting along?" I asked, on coming home at night.

"Humph! Not getting along at all!" replied Mrs. Sunderland, in a fretful tone. "In two days, the girls might have thoroughly cleaned the house from top to bottom, and what do you think they have done? Nothing at all!"

"Nothing at all! They must have done something."

"Well, next to nothing, then. They havn't finished the front and back chambers. And what is worse, Ann has gone away sick, and Hannah is in bed with a real or pretended sick-headache."

"Oh, dear!" I ejaculated, involuntarily.

"Now, a'nt things in a pretty way?"

"I think they are," I replied, and then asked, "what are you going to do?"

"I have sent John for old Jane, who helped us to clean house last spring. But, as likely as not, she's at work somewhere."

Such was in fact the case, for John came in a moment after with that consoling report.

"Go and see Nancy, then," my wife said, sharply, to John, as if he were to blame for Jane's being at work.

John turned away slowly and went on his errand, evidently in not the most amiable mood in the world. It was soon ascertained that Nancy couldn't come.

"Why can't she come?" enquired my wife.

"She says she's doing some sewing for herself, and can't go out this week," replied John.

"Go and tell her that she must come. That my house is upside down, and both the girls are sick."

But Nancy was in no mood to comply. John brought back another negative.

"Go and say to her, John, that I will not take no for an answer: that she must come. I will give her a dollar a day."

This liberal offer of a dollar a day was effective. Nancy came and went, to work on the next morning. Of course, Ann did not come back; and as it was Hannah's last day, she felt privileged to have more headache than was consistent with cleaning paint or scrubbing floors. The work went on, therefore, very slowly.

Saturday night found us without cook or chamber-maid, and with only two rooms in order in the whole house, viz. our chambers on the second story. By great persuasion, Nancy was induced to stay during Sunday and cook for us.

An advertisement in the newspaper on Monday morning, brought us a couple of raw Irish girls, who were taken as better than nobody at all. With these new recruits, Mrs. Sunderland set about getting "things to right." Nancy plodded on, so well pleased with her wages, that she continued to get the work of one day lengthened out into two, and so managed to get a week's job.

For the whole of another precious week we were in confusion.

"How do your new girls get along?" I asked of my wife, upon whose face I had not seen a smile for ten days.

T. S. Arthur

"Don't name them, Mr. Sunderland! They're not worth the powder it would take to shoot them. Lazy, ignorant, dirty, good-for-nothing creatures. I wouldn't give them house-room."

"I'm sorry to learn that. What will you do?" I said.

"Dear knows! I was so well suited in Ann and Hannah, and, to think that they should have served me so! I wouldn't have believed it of them. But they are all as destitute of feeling and principle as they can be. And John continues as sulky as a bear. He pretended to shake the carpets but you might get a wheelbarrow-load of dirt out of them. I told him so, and the impudent follow replied that he didn't know any thing about shaking carpets; and that it wasn't the waiter's place, any how."

"He did?"

"Yes, he did. I was on the eve of ordering him to leave the house."

"I'll save you that trouble," I said, a little warmly.

"Don't say any thing to him, if you please, Mr. Sunderland," returned my wife. "There couldn't be a better man about the house than he is, for all ordinary purposes. If we should lose him, we shall never get another half so good. I wish I'd hired a man to shake the carpets at once; they would have been much better done, and I should have had John's cheerful assistance about the house, which would have been a great deal."

That evening I overheard, accidentally, a conversation between John and the new girls, which threw some light upon the whole matter.

"John," said one of them, "what made Mrs. Sunderland's cook and chamber maid go aff and lave her right in the middle of house-clainin'?"

"Because Mrs. Sunderland, instead of hiring a woman, as every lady does, tried to put it all off upon them."

"Indade! and was that it?"

"Yes, it was. They never thought of leaving until they found they were to be imposed upon; and, to save fifty cents or a dollar, she made me shake the carpets. I never did such a thing in my life before. I think I managed to leave about as much dirt in as I shook out. But I'll leave the house before I do it again."

"So would I, John. It was downright mane imposition, so it was. Set a waiter to shaking carpets!"

"I don't think much has been saved," remarked the waiter, "for Nancy has had a dollar a day ever since she has been here."

"Indade!"

"Yes; and besides that, Mrs. Sunderland has had to work like a dog herself. All this might have been saved, if she had hired a couple of women at sixty-two and a half cents a day for two or three days, and paid for having the carpets shaken; that's the way other people do. The house would have been set to rights in three or four days, and every thing going on like clockwork."

"I heard no more. I wanted to hear no more; it was all as clear as day to me. When I related to Mrs. Sunderland what John had said, she was, at first, quite indignant. But the reasonableness of the thing soon became so apparent that she could not but acknowledge that she had acted very unwisely.

"This is another specimen of your saving at the spigot," I said, playfully.

"There, Mr. Sunderland! not a word more, if you please, of that," she returned, her cheek more flushed than usual. "It is my duty, as your wife, to dispense with prudence in your household; and if, in seeking to do so, I have run a little into extremes, I think it ill becomes you to ridicule or censure me. Dear knows! I have not sought my own ease or comfort in the matter."

"My dear, good wife," I quickly said, in a soothing voice, "I have neither meant to ridicule nor censure you - nothing was farther from my thoughts."

"You shall certainly have no cause to complain of me on this score again," she said, still a little warmly. "When next we clean house, I will take care that it shall be done by extra help altogether."

"Do, so by all means, Mrs. Sunderland. Let there be, if possible, two paint-cleaners and scrubbers in every room, that the work may all be done in a day instead of a week. Take my word for it, the cost will be less; or, if double, I will cheerfully pay it for the sake of seeing 'order from chaos rise' more quickly than is wont under the ordinary system of doing things."

My wife did not just like this speech, I could see, but she bit her lips and kept silent.

In a week we were without a cook again; and months passed before we were in any thing like domestic comfort. At last my wife was fortunate enough to get Ann and Hannah back again, and then the old pleasant order of things was restored. I rather think that we shall have a different state of things at next house-cleaning time. I certainly hope so.

CHAPTER XVII

BROILING A LOBSTER

MR. SMITH'S appetite sometimes takes an epicurean turn, and then we indulge in a lobster, calf's-head soup, terrapins, or something of that sort.

Once upon a time, he sent home a lobster. I did not feel very well that day, and concluded to leave the cooking of the animal to a new girl that I had taken a week or two before, on a strong recommendation. She claimed to be a finished cook, and her testimonials were distinct on that head.

"Kitty," said I, "Mr. Smith has sent home a lobster, I believe?"

I had summoned the girl to my room.

"Yes, ma'am," she replied. "Is it for dinner?"

"Of course it is; and you must see that it is well cooked."

Kitty lingered a few moments, as if not entirely satisfied about something, and then retired to the kitchen.

"I wonder if she knows how to boil a lobster?" said I to myself.

But then, the remembrance that she had come to me as a finished cook, crossed my mind, and I answered, mentally, my own question, by saying:

T. S. Arthur

"Of course she does."

Not long afterwards, I went to the dining-room, which was over the kitchen. I had been there only a little while, when I heard an unusual noise below, followed by an exclamation from Kitty -

"Oh! murderation! I can't cook the straddling thing. I wonder what Mr. Smith brought it home alive for!"

I was, of course, all attention now, and going to the top of the stairs, stood listening to what was going on below.

"There now. Lie still!" I heard Kitty say. This was followed by a rattling of tongs, or some other iron implements, and a rapid shuffling of feet.

Curious to know what was going on, I stepped lightly down the stairs, and through the open door had a full view of both Kitty and the lobster.

Live coals had been raked out upon the hearth. Over these was placed a gridiron, and on this not very comfortable bed Kitty was endeavoring to force Mr. Lobster to lie still and be cooked. But this he was by no means inclined to do; and no sooner did she place him on the heated bars, than he made his way off in the quickest possible time. Then she caught hold of him with the tongs, restored him to his proper position on the gridiron, and with poker and tongs strove to hold him there.

As the lobster, a second and a third time, struggled free of Kitty's tongs and poker, I could no longer restrain myself, but burst forth into a loud fit of laughter. By the time this subsided, his lobstership was in the middle of the kitchen floor. Picking him up, I threw him into a pot of boiling water, and then retreated from the kitchen, so convulsed with laughter that I could not utter a word.

Kitty did not soon hear the last of her attempt to broil a lobster.

T. S. Arthur

CHAPTER XVIII

THE STRAWBERRY-WOMAN

THE observance of economy in matters of family expenditure, is the duty of every housekeeper. But, there is an economy that involves wrong to others, which, as being unjust and really dishonest, should be carefully avoided. In a previous chapter, I introduced the, story of a poor fish-woman, as affording a lesson for the humane. Let me here give another, which forcibly illustrates the subject of oppressive and unjust economy. It is the story of a "Strawberry-Woman," and appeared in one of the magazines some years ago.

"Strawb'*rees!* Strawb'*rees!* cried a poorly clad, tired-looking woman, about eleven o clock one sultry June morning. She was passing a handsome house in Walnut street, into the windows of which she looked earnestly, in the hope of seeing the face of a customer. She did not look in vain, for the shrill sound of her voice brought forward a lady, dressed in a silk morning-wrapper, who beckoned her to stop. The woman lifted the heavy, tray from her bead, and placing it upon the door-step, sat wearily down.

"What's the price of your strawberries?" asked the lady, as she came to the door.

"Ten cents a box, madam. They are right fresh."

"Ten cents!" replied the lady, in a tone of surprise, drawing herself up, and looking grave. Then shaking her head and compressing her lips firmly, she added:

"I can't give ten cents for strawberries. It's too much."

"You can't get such strawberries as these for less, madam," said the woman. "I got a levy a box for them yesterday."

"Then you got too much, that's all I have to say. I never pay such prices. I bought strawberries in the market yesterday, just as good as yours, for eight cents a box."

"Don't know how they do to sell them at that price," returned the woman. "Mine cost nearly eight cents, and ought to bring me at least twelve. But I am willing to take ten, so that I can, sell out quickly. It's a very hot day." And the woman wiped, with her apron, the perspiration from her glowing face.

"No, I won't pay ten cents," said the lady (?) coldly. "I'll give you forty cents for five boxes, and nothing more."

"But, madam, they cost me within a trifle of eight cents a box."

"I can't help that. You paid too much for them, and this must be your loss, not mine, if I buy your strawberries. I never pay for other people's mistakes. I understand the use of money much better than that."

The poor woman did not feel very well. The day was unusually hot and sultry, and her tray felt heavier, and tired her more than usual. Five boxes would lighten it, and if she sold her berries at eight cents, she would clear two cents and a half, and that would be better than nothing.

"I'll tell you what I will do," she said, after thinking a few moments; "I don't feel as well as usual to-day, and my tray is heavy. Five boxes sold will be something. You shall have them at nine cents. They cost me seven and a half, and I'm sure it's worth a cent and a half a box to cry them about the streets such hot weather as this."

"I have told you, my good woman, exactly what I will do," said the customer, with dignity. "If you are willing to take what I offer you, say so; if not, we needn't stand here any longer."

"Well, I suppose you will have to take them," replied the strawberry-woman, seeing that there was no hope of doing better. "But it's too little."

"It's enough," said the lady, as she turned to call a servant. Five boxes of fine large strawberries were received, and forty cents paid for them. The lady re-entered the parlor, pleased at her good bargain, while the poor woman turned from the door sad and disheartened. She walked nearly the distance of a square before she could trust her voice to utter her monotonous cry of

"Strawb'*rees!* Strawb'*rees!*"

An hour afterward, a friend called upon Mrs. Mier, the lady who had bought the strawberries. After talking about various matters and things interesting to lady housekeepers, Mrs. Mier said:

"How much did you pay for strawberries this morning?"

"Ten cents."

"You paid too much. I bought them for eight."

"For eight! Were they good ones?"

"Step into the dining-room, and I will show them to you."

The ladies stepped into the dining-room, when Mrs. Mier displayed her large, red berries, which were really much finer than she had at first supposed them to be.

"You didn't get them for eight cents," remarked the visitor, incredulously.

"Yes I did. I paid forty cents for five boxes."

"While I paid fifty for some not near so good."

"I suppose you paid just what you were asked?"

"Yes, I always do that. I buy from one woman during the season, who agrees to furnish me at the regular market price."

"Which you will always find to be two or three cents above what you can get them for in the market."

"You always buy in market."

"I bought these from a woman at the door."

"Did she only ask eight cents for them?"

"Oh, no! She asked ten cents, and pretended that she got twelve and a half for the same quality of berries yesterday. But I never give these people what they ask."

"While I never can find it in my heart to ask a poor, tired-looking woman at my door, to take a cent less for her fruit than she asks me. A cent or two, while it is of little account to me, must be of great importance to her."

"You are a very poor economist, I see," said Mrs. Mier. "If that is the way you deal with every one, your husband no doubt finds his expense account a very serious item."

"I don't know about that. He never complains. He allows me a certain sum every week to keep the house, and find my own and the children's clothes; and so far from ever calling on him for more, I always have fifty or a hundred dollars lying by me."

"You must have a precious large allowance, then, considering your want of economy in paying everybody just what they ask for their things."

"Oh, no! I don't do that, exactly, Mrs. Mier. If I consider the price of a thing too high, I don't buy it."

"You paid too high for your strawberries today."

"Perhaps I did; although I am by no means certain."

"You can judge for yourself. Mine cost but eight cents, and you own that they are superior to yours at ten cents."

"Still, yours may have been too cheap, instead of mine too dear."

"Too cheap! That is funny! I never saw any thing too cheap in my life. The great trouble is, that every thing is too dear. What do you mean by too cheap?"

"The person who sold them to you may not have made profit enough upon them to pay for her time and labor. If this were the case, she sold them to you too cheap."

"Suppose she paid too high for them? Is the purchaser to pay for her error?"

"Whether she did so, it would be hard to tell; and even if she had made such a mistake, I think it would be more just and humane to pay her a price that would give her a fair profit, instead of taking from her the means of buying bread for her children. At least, this is my way of reasoning."

"And a precious lot of money it must take to support such a system of reasoning. But how much, pray, do you have a week to keep the family? I am curious to know."

"Thirty-five dollars."

"Thirty-five dollars! You are jesting."

"Oh, no! That is exactly what I receive, and as I have said, I find the sum ample."

"While I receive fifty dollars a week," said Mrs. Mier, "and am forever calling on my husband to settle some bill or other for me. And yet I never pay the exorbitant prices asked by everybody for every thing. I am strictly economical in my family. While other people pay their domestics a dollar and a half and two dollars a week, I give but a dollar and a quarter each to my cook and chambermaid, and require the chamber maid to help the washer-woman on Mondays. Nothing is wasted in my kitchen, for I take care in marketing, not to allow room for waste. I don't know how it is that you save money on thirty-five dollars with your system, while I find fifty dollars inadequate with my system."

The exact difference in the two systems will be clearly understood by the reader, when he is informed that although Mrs. Mier never paid any body as much as was at first asked for an article, and was always talking about economy, and trying to practice it, by withholding from others what was justly their due, as in the case of the strawberry-woman, yet she was a very extravagant person, and spared no money in gratifying her own pride. Mrs. Gilman, her visitor, was, on the contrary, really economical, because she was moderate in all her desires, and was usually as well satisfied with an article of dress or furniture that cost ten or twenty dollars, as Mrs. Mier was with one that cost forty or fifty dollars. In little things, the former was not so particular as to infringe the rights of others, while in larger matters, she was careful not to run into extravagance in order to gratify her own or children's pride and vanity, while the latter pursued a course directly opposite.

Mrs. Gilman was not as much dissatisfied, on reflection, about the price she had paid for her strawberries, as she had felt at first.

T. S. Arthur

"I would rather pay these poor creatures two cents a box too much than too little," she said to herself - "dear knows, they earn their money hard enough, and get but a scanty portion after all."

Although the tray of the poor strawberry-woman, when she passed from the presence of Mrs. Mier, was lighter by five boxes, her heart was heavier, and that made her steps more weary than before. The next place at which she stopped, she found the same disposition to beat her down in her price.

"I'll give you nine cents, and take four boxes," said the lady.

"Indeed, madam, that is too little," replied the woman; "ten cents is the lowest at which I can sell them and make even a reasonable profit."

"Well, say thirty-seven and a half for four boxes, and I will take them. It is only two cents and a half less than you ask for them."

"Give me a fip, ma! - there comes the candy-man!" exclaimed a little fellow, pressing up to the side of the lady. "Quick, ma! Here, candy-man!" calling after an old man with a tin cylinder under his arm, that looked something like an ice cream freezer. The lady drew out her purse, and searched among its contents for the small coin her child wanted.

"I havn't any thing less than a levy," she at length said.

"Oh, well, he can change it. Candy-man, you can change a levy?"

By this time the "candy-man" stood smiling beside the strawberry-woman. As he was counting out the fip's worth of candy, the child spoke up in an earnest voice, and said:

"Get a levy's worth, mother, do, wont you? Cousin Lu's coming to see us to-morrow."

"Let him have a levy's worth, candy-man. He's such a rogue I can't resist him," responded the mother. The candy was counted out, and the levy paid, when the man retired in his usual good humor.

"Shall I take these strawberries for thirty-seven and a half cents?" said the lady, the smile fading from her face. "It is all I am willing to give."

"If you wont pay any more, I musn't stand for two cents and a half," replied the woman, "although they would nearly buy a loaf of bread for the children," she mentally added.

The four boxes were sold for the sum offered, and the woman lifted the tray upon her head, and moved on again. The sun shone out still hotter and hotter as the day advanced. Large beads of perspiration rolled from the throbbing temples of the strawberry-woman, as she passed wearily up one street and down another, crying her fruit at the top of her voice. At length all were sold but five boxes, and now it was past one o'clock. Long before this she ought to have been at home. Faint from over-exertion, she lifted her tray from her head, and placing it upon a door-step, sat down to rest. As she sat thus, a lady came up, and paused at the door of the house, as if about to enter.

"You look tired, my good woman," she said kindly. "This is a very hot day for such hard work as yours. How do you sell your strawberries?"

"I ought to have ten cents for them, but nobody seems willing to give ten cents to-day, although they are very fine, and cost me as much as some I have got twelve and a half for."

"How many boxes have you?"

"Five, ma'am."

"They are very fine, sure enough," said the lady, stooping

down and examining them; "and well worth ten cents. I'll take them."

"Thanky, ma'am. I was afraid I should have to take them home," said the woman, her heart bounding up lightly.

The lady rung the bell, for it was at her door that the tired strawberry-woman had stopped to rest herself. While she was waiting for the door to be opened, the lady took from her purse the money for the strawberries, and handing it to the woman, said:

"Here is your money. Shall I tell the servant to bring you out a glass of cool water? You are hot and tired."

"If you please, ma'am," said the woman, with a grateful look.

The water was sent out by the servant who was to receive the strawberries, and the tired woman drank it eagerly. Its refreshing coolness flowed through every vein, and when she took up her tray to return home, both heart and step were lighter.

The lady whose benevolent feelings had prompted her to the performance of this little act of kindness, could not help remembering the woman's grateful look. She had not done much - not more than it was every one's duty to do; but the recollection of even that was pleasant, far more pleasant than could possibly have been Mrs. Mier's self-gratulations at having saved ten cents on her purchase of five boxes of strawberries, notwithstanding the assurance of the poor woman who vended them, that, at the reduced rate, her profit on the whole would only be two cents and a half.

After dinner Mrs. Mier went out and spent thirty dollars in purchasing jewelry for her eldest daughter, a young lady not yet eighteen years of age. That evening, at the tea-table, the strawberries were highly commended as being the largest and most delicious in flavor of any they had yet had; in reply to which, Mrs. Mier stated, with an air of peculiar satisfaction, that she had got them for eight cents a box, when they were worth at least ten cents.

"The woman asked me ten cents," she said, "but I offered her eight, and she took them."

While the family of Mrs. Mier were enjoying their pleasant repast, the strawberry-woman sat at a small table, around which were gathered three young children, the oldest but six years of age. She had started out in the morning with thirty boxes of strawberries, for which she was to pay seven and a half cents a box. If all had brought the ten cents a box, she would have made seventy-five cents; but such was not the case. Rich ladies had beaten her down in her price - had chaffered with her for the few pennies of profits to which her hard labor entitled her - and actually robbed her of the meager pittance she strove to earn for her children. Instead of realizing the small sum of seventy-five cents, she had cleared only forty-five cents. With this she bought a little Indian meal and molasses for her own and her children's supper and breakfast.

As she sat with her children, eating the only food she was able to provide for them, and thought of what had occurred during the day, a feeling of bitterness toward her kind came over her; but the remembrance of the kind words, and the glass of cool water, so timely and thoughtfully tendered to her, was like leaves in the waters of Marah. Her heart softened, and with the tears stealing to her eyes, she glanced upward, and asked a blessing on her who had remembered that, though poor, she was still human.

Economy is a good thing, and should be practiced by all, but it should show itself in denying ourselves, not in oppressing others. We see persons spending dollar after dollar foolishly one hour, and in the next trying to save a five penny piece off of a wood-sawyer, coal-heaver, or market-woman. Such things are disgraceful, if not dishonest.

T. S. Arthur

CHAPTER XIX

LOTS OF THINGS

"O DEAR!" said I to Mr. Smith one morning, as we arose from the breakfast-table, at which we had been partaking of rather a badly-cooked meal, - "more trouble in prospect."

"What's the matter now?" asked Mr. Smith, with a certain emphasis on the word "now" that didn't sound just agreeable to my ears.

"Oh, nothing! nothing!" I answered, with as much indifference of manner as I could assume.

"You spoke of trouble," said he, kindly, "and trouble, in my experience, is rather more tangible than 'nothing.'"

"I've another raw Irish girl in the kitchen, who, according to her own confession, hasn't been above ten days in the country. Isn't that enough?"

"I should think so. But, why, in the name of goodness did you take another of these green islanders into your house?"

"It's easy enough to ask questions, Mr. Smith," said I, a little fretfully; "but - " I checked myself. We looked at each other, smiled, and - said no more on the subject.

"Your name is Anna, I believe?" said I, as I stepped to the

kitchen-door, a couple of hours afterwards.

"Thot's me name," replied the new domestic.

"I will send home a loin of veal and some green peas," said I. "They are for dinner, which must be ready at two o'clock. You know how to roast a piece of veal, I presume?"

"Lave me for thot same, honey!"

"And the green peas?"

"All right, mum. I've lived in quality houses since I was so high. I can cook ony thing."

"Very well, Anna. We will see. I have to go out this morning; and you must do the best you can. Don't fail to have dinner ready by two o'clock. Mr. Smith is a punctual man."

Anna was profuse in her promises.

"If," said I, recollecting myself, as I was about opening the street door, and returning along the passage, - "If any thing is sent home for me, be sure to take it up stairs and lay it carefully on my bed."

"Yes, mum."

"Now don't forget this, Anna."

"Och! niver fear a hate, mum," was the girl's answer. "I'll not forget a word iv y'r insthructions."

I turned away and left the house. My principal errand was a visit to the milliner's, where I wished to see a bonnet I had ordered, before it was sent home. It was this bonnet I referred to when I desired Anna to place carefully on the bed in my chamber, any thing that might come home.

T. S. Arthur

On my way to the milliner's, I stopped at the grocer's where we were in the habit of dealing, and made selections of various things that were needed.

The bonnet proved just to my taste. It was a delicate white spring bonnet, with a neat trimming, and pleased my fancy wonderfully.

"The very thing," said I, the moment my eyes rested upon it.

"Do you want a box?" asked the milliner, after I had decided to take the bonnet.

"I have one," was my answer.

"O, very well. I will send the bonnet home in a box, and you can take it out."

"That will do."

"Shall I send it home this morning?"

"If you please."

"Very well. I'll see that it is done."

After this I made a number of calls, which occupied me until after one o'clock, when I turned my face homeward. On arriving, I was admitted by my new girl, and, as the thought of my beautiful bonnet now returned to my mind, my first words were:

"Has any thing been sent home for me, Anna?"

"Och! yis indade, mum," was her answer, - "lots o' things."

"Lots of things!" said I, with manifest surprise; for I only remembered at the moment my direction to the milliner to send home my bonnet.

"Yis, indade!" responded the girl. "Lots. And the mon brought 'em on the funniest whale barry ye iver seed."

"On a wheel barrow!"

"Yis. And such a whale barry! It had a whale on each side, as I'm a livin' sinner, mum and a cunnin' little whale in front, cocked 'way up intil the air, thot didn't touch nothin' at all - at all! There's no sich whale barrys as thot same in Ireland, me leddy!"

"And what did you do with the lots of things brought on this wheel barrow?" said I, now beginning to comprehend the girl.

"Put them on y'r bed, sure."

"On my bed!" I exclaimed, in consternation.

"Sure, and didn't I remember the last words ye spake till me? 'Anna,' says ye, - 'Anna, if ony thing is sent home for me, be sure till take it carefully up stairs and lay it on me bed.' And I did thot same. Sure, I couldn't have found a nicer place, if I gone the house over."

Turning from the girl, I hurried up stairs.

It was as I had too good reason to fear. Such a sight as met my eyes! In the centre of my bed, with its snowy-white Marseilles covering, were piled "lots of things," and no mistake. Sugar, tea, cheese, coffee, soap, and various other articles, not excepting a bottle of olive oil, from the started cork of which was gently oozing a slender stream, lay in a jumbled heap; while, on a satin damask-covered chair, reposed a greasy ham. For a moment I stood confounded. Then, giving the bell a violent jerk, I awaited, in angry impatience, the appearance of Anna, who, in due time, after going to the street door, found her way to my chamber.

"Anna!" I exclaimed, "what, in the name of goodness,

possessed you to do this?"

And I pointed to the bed.

"Sure, and ye towld me till put them on ye's bed."

"I told you no such thing, you stupid creature! I said if a bonnet came, to put it on the bed."

"Och! sorry a word did ye iver say about a bonnet, mum. It's the first time I iver heard ony thing about a bonnet from yer blessed lips. And thot's thrue."

"Where is my bonnet, then? Did one come home?"

"Plase, mum, and there did. And a purty one it is, too, as iver my two eyes looked upon."

"What did you do with it?" I enquired, with a good deal of concern.

"It's safe in thot great mahogany closet, mum," she replied, pointing to my wardrobe.

I stepped quickly to the "mahogany closet," and threw open the door. Alas! for my poor bonnet! It was crushed in between two of Mr. Smith's coats, and tied to a peg, by the strings, which were, of course, crumpled to a degree that made them useless.

"Too bad! Too bad!" I murmured, as I disengaged the bonnet from its unhappy companionship with broadcloth. As it came to the light, my eyes fell upon two dark spots on the front, the unmistakable prints of Anna's greasy fingers. This was too much! I tossed it, in a moment of passion, upon the bed, where, in contact with the "lots of things," it received its final touch of ruin from a portion of the oozing contents of the sweet oil bottle.

Of the scene that followed, and of the late, badly-cooked dinner to which my husband was introduced an hour afterwards, I will not trust myself to write. I was not, of course, in a very agreeable humor; and the record of what I said and did, and of how I looked, would be in no way flattering to my own good opinion of myself, nor prove particularly edifying to the reader.

I shall never forget Anna's new variety of "whale-barry," nor the "lots o' things" she deposited on my bed. She lived with me just seven days, and then made way for another a little more tolerable than herself.

T. S. Arthur

CHAPTER XX

A CURE FOR LOW SPIRITS

FROM some cause, real or imaginary, I felt low spirited. There was a cloud upon my feelings, and I could not smile as usual, nor speak in a tone of cheerfulness. As a natural result, the light of my countenance being gone, all things around me were in a shadow. My husband was sober, and had but little to say; the children would look strangely at me when I answered their questions or spoke to them for any purpose, and the domestics moved about in a quiet manner, and when they addressed me, did so in a tone more subdued than usual.

This reaction upon my state, only made darker the clouds that veiled my spirits. I was conscious of this, and was conscious that the original cause of depression was entirely inadequate, in itself, to produce the result which had followed. Under this feeling, I made an effort to rally myself, but in vain - and sank lower from the struggle to rise above the gloom that overshadowed me.

When my husband came home at dinner time, I tried to meet him with a smile; but I felt that the light upon my countenance was feeble, and of brief duration. He looked at me earnestly, and in his kind and gentle way, enquired if I felt no better, affecting to believe that my ailment was one of the body instead of the mind. But I scarcely answered him, and I could see that he felt hurt. How, much more wretched did I become at this? Could I have then retired to my chamber, and alone given my heart full vent in a passion of tears, I might have obtained relief to my feelings. But I could not do this.

While I sat at the table forcing a little food into my mouth for appearance sake, my husband said:

"You remember the fine lad who has been with me for some time?"

I nodded my head, but the question did not awaken in my mind the least interest.

"He has not made his appearance for several days; and I learned this morning, on sending to the house of his mother, that he is very ill."

"Ah!" was my indifferent response. Had I spoken, what was in my mind, I would have said, "I'm sorry, but I can't help it." I did not at the moment feel the smallest interest in the lad.

"Yes," added my husband, "and the person who called to let me know about it, expressed his fears that Edward would not get up again."

"What ails him?" I enquired.

"I did not clearly understand. But he has a fever of some kind. You remember his mother very well?"

"Oh, yes. You know she worked for me. Edward is her only child, I believe."

"Yes; and his loss to her will be almost everything."

"Is he dangerous?" I enquired, a feeling of interest beginning to stir in my heart.

"He is not expected to live."

T. S. Arthur

"Poor woman! How distressed she must be! I wonder what her circumstances are just at this time. She seemed very poor when she worked for me."

"And she is very poor still, I doubt not. She has herself been sick, and during the time it is more than probable that Edward's wages were all her income. I am afraid she has not now the means of procuring for her sick boy things necessary for his comfort. Could you not go around there this afternoon, and see how they are?"

I shook my head instantly at this proposition, for sympathy for others was not strong enough to expel my selfish despondency of mind.

"Then I must step around," replied my husband, "before I go back to business, although I have a great deal to do to-day. It would not be right to neglect this lad and his mother under present circumstances."

I felt rebuked at these words, and, with an effort, said:

"I will go."

"It will be much better for you to see them than for me," returned my husband, "for you can understand their wants better, and minister to them more effectually. If they need any comforts, I would like to have you see them supplied."

It still cost me an effort to get ready, but as I had promised to do as my husband wished, the effort had to be made. By the time I was prepared to go out, I felt something better. The exertion I was required to make, tended to disperse, slightly, the clouds that hung over me, and as they began gradually to remove, my thoughts turned, with an awakened interest, towards the object of my husban d's solicitude.

All was silent within the humble abode to which my errand led me. I knocked lightly, and in a few moments the mother of

Edward opened the door. She looked pale and anxious.

"How is your son, Mrs. Ellis?" I enquired, as I stepped in.

"He is very low, ma'am," she replied.

"Not dangerous, I hope?"

"The fever has left him, but he is as weak as an infant. All his strength is gone."

"But proper nourishment will restore him, now that the disease is broken."

"So the doctor says. But I'm afraid it's too late. He seems to be sinking every hour. Will you walk up and see him?"

I followed Mrs. Ellis up stairs, and into a chamber, where the sick boy lay. I was not surprised at the fear she expressed, when I saw Edward's pale, sunken face, and hollow, almost expressionless eyes. He scarcely noticed my entrance.

"Poor boy!" sighed his mother. "He has had a very sick spell."

My liveliest interest was at once awakened.

"He has been sick, indeed!" I replied, as I laid my hand upon his white forehead.

I found his skin cold and damp. The fever had nearly burned out the vital energy of his system.

"Do you give him much nourishment?"

"He takes a little barley-water."

"Has not the doctor ordered wine?"

"Yes, ma'am," replied Mrs. Ellis, but she spoke with an air of

T. S. Arthur

hesitation. "He says a spoonful of good wine, three or four times a day, would be very good for him."

"And you have not given him any?"

"No, ma'am."

"We have some very pure wine, that we always keep for sickness. If you will step over to our house, and tell Alice to give you a bottle of it, I will stay with Edward until you return."

How brightly glowed that poor woman's face as my words fell upon her ears!

"O, ma'am, you are very kind!" said she. "But it will be asking too much of you to stay here!"

"You didn't ask it, Mrs. Ellis," I simply replied. "I have offered to stay; so do you go for the wine as quickly as you can, for Edward needs it very much."

I was not required to say more. In a few minutes I was alone with the sick boy, who lay almost as still as if death were resting upon his half-closed eye-lids. To some extent during the half hour I remained thus in that hushed chamber, did I realize the condition and feelings of the poor mother, whose only son lay gasping at the very door of death, and all my sympathies were, in consequence, awakened.

As soon as Mrs. Ellis returned with the wine, about a teaspoonful was diluted, and the glass containing it placed to the sick lad's lips. The moment its flavor touched his palate, a thrill seemed to pass through his frame, and he swallowed eagerly.

"It does him good!" said I, speaking warmly, and from an impulse that made my heart glow.

We sat and looked with silent interest upon the boy's face, and we did not look in vain, for something like warmth came upon his wan cheeks, and when I placed my hand upon his forehead, the coldness and dampness were gone. The wine had quickened his languid pulse. I stayed an hour longer, and then another spoonful of the generous wine was given. Its effect was as marked as the first. I then withdrew from the humble home of the widow and her only child, promising to see them again in the morning.

When I regained the street, and my thoughts for a moment reverted to myself, how did I find all changed? The clouds had been dispersed - the heavy load had been raised from my bosom. I walked with a free step.

Sympathy for others, and active efforts to do others good, had expelled the evil spirit from my heart; and now serene peace had there again her quiet habitation. There was light in every part of my dwelling when I re-entered it, and I sung cheerfully, as I prepared with my own hands, a basket of provisions for the poor widow.

When my husband returned again in the evening, he found me at work, cheerfully, in my family, and all bright and smiling again. The efforts to do good to others had driven away the darkness from my spirit, and the sunshine was again on my countenance, and reflected from every member of my household.

T. S. Arthur

CHAPTER XXI

A BARGAIN

I AM not much of a bargain-buyer, having had, like most housekeepers, sufficient experience on that subject to effect a pretty thorough cure of the disease, mild as it was in the beginning. As all diseases, whether bodily or mental, leave behind them a predisposition to return, I have, from time to time, been subjected to slight paroxisms of the old complaint. From the effects of my last rather mild attack, I am now recovering.

I was passing along Walnut street, on my way to drop a letter in the Post Office, one morning, about ten o'clock, when the ringing of an auctioneer's bell came suddenly on my ears. Lifting my eyes, I saw the flag of Thomas & Son displayed before me, and read the words, "Auction this morning."

Here was an "exciting cause," as the doctors say, and, instantly I felt a movement of the old affection. Two or three ladies happened to be entering the store at the time, and the sudden inclination to follow them was so strong that I did not attempt its resistance. It was not my intention, to buy any thing, of course; for I was conscious of no particular want. I only just wished, if any wish were really full formed, to see what was to be sold.

Scarcely had I entered the door, when a sofa, so nearly new that it hardly bore a mark of having been used, presented itself, and captivated my fancy. The one that graced our parlor had grown somewhat out of fashion. It was in good keeping, but rather plain in style: and, as we had recently treated ourselves to handsome new carpets, did not appear to quite so good advantage as before. This one, to be sold at auction, was made after a newer pattern, and, as my eyes continued to rest upon it, the desires to have it in my parlor was fully formed.

I have said, that on entering the auction store, I was unconscious of any particular want. This was true, notwithstanding Mr. Smith and I had, a few days before, called at a cabinet maker's wareroom, to look at a sofa. In consequence of former experience in cheap furniture, we had no thought of getting a low-priced article from a second or third rate establishment; but designed, when we did purchase, to act wisely and get the best. We had been looking at a sofa for which sixty-five dollars was asked; and were hesitating between that and another upon which fifty dollars was set as the price.

It was but natural, under these circumstances, that I should, look upon this sofa with more than ordinary interest. A glance told me that it was an article of superior make, and a close examination fully confirmed this impression.

A few minutes after my entrance, the sale begun, and it so happened that the sofa came first on the list.

"We shall begin this morning," said the auctioneer, "with a superior, fashionable sofa, made by -. It has only been in use a short time, and is, in every respect, equal to new."

All my predilections in favor of the sofa were confirmed the moment the manufacturer's name was announced. Of course, it was of the best material and workmanship.

"What is bid for this superior sofa, made by - ," went on the salesman, - "Seventy dollars - sixty-five - sixty-fifty - five-fifty - forty-five - forty - thirty-five - thirty."

T. S. Arthur

"Twenty-five dollars," said a timid voice.

"Twenty-five! Twenty-five!" cried the auctioneer.

"Twenty-six," said I.

The first bidder advanced a dollar on this; then I bid twenty-eight; he went up to twenty-nine, and I made it thirty, at which offer the sofa was knocked down to me.

"That's a bargain, and no mistake," said the salesman. "It is worth fifty dollars, if it's worth a cent."

"I'll give you five dollars advance," proposed a lady by my side, who had desired to bid, but could not bring up her courage to the point.

"No, thank you," was my prompt answer. I was too well pleased with my bargain.

When Mr. Smith came home to dinner on that day, I met him in the parlor.

"What do you think of this?" said I, pointing to the new sofa. I spoke in an exultant voice.

"Where in the world did it come from?" enquired Mr. Smith, evincing a natural surprise.

"I bought it," was my reply.

"When? where?"

"This morning, at auction."

"At auction!"

"Yes; and it's a bargain. Now guess what I gave for it?"

"Ten dollars?"

"Now Mr. Smith! But come; be serious. Isn't it cheap at forty dollars?"

Mr. Smith examined the sofa with care, and then gave it as his opinion that it wasn't dear at forty dollars.

"I got it for thirty," said I.

"Indeed! I should really call that a bargain, - provided you don't discover in it, after a while, some defect."

"I've looked at every part, over and over again," was my response to this, "and can find a defect nowhere. None exists, I am satisfied."

"Time will show," remarked Mr. Smith.

There was the smallest perceptible doubt in his tone.

Next morning, on going into my parlors, I was a little worried to see two or three moths flying about the room. They were despatched with commendable quickness. On the morning that followed, the same thing occurred again; and this was repeated, morning after morning. Moreover, in a few days, these insects, so dreaded by housekeepers, showed themselves in the chambers above. Up to this time I had neglected to put away my furs, a new set of which had been purchased during the previous winter. I delayed this no longer.

House-cleaning time had now arrived. My new carpets were taken up and packed away, to give place to the cooler matting. Our winter clothing also received attention, and was deposited in chests and closets for the summer, duly provided with all needful protection from moths. After this came the calm of rest and self-satisfaction.

One day, about the middle of July, a lady friend called in to

T. S. Arthur

see me.

"That's a neat sofa, Mrs. Smith," said she, in the pause of a conversation.

"I think it very neat," was my answer.

"It's made from the same pattern with one that I had. One that I always liked, and from which I was sorry to part."

"You sold it?" said I.

"Yes. I sent it to auction."

"Ah! Why so?"

"I discovered, this spring, that the moth had got into it."

"Indeed!"

"Yes. They showed themselves, every day, in such numbers, in my parlors, that I became alarmed for my carpets. I soon traced their origin to the sofa, which was immediately packed off to auction. I was sorry to part with it; but, there was no other effective remedy."

"You lost on the sale, I presume," I ventured to remark.

"Yes; that was to be expected. It cost sixty dollars, and brought only thirty. But this loss was to be preferred to the destruction such an army of moth as it was sending forth, would have occasioned."

I changed the subject, dexterously, having heard quite enough about the sofa to satisfy me that my bargain was likely to prove a bad one.

All the summer, I was troubled with visions of moth-eaten carpets, furs, shawls, and overcoats; and they proved to be only the foreshadowing of real things to come, for, when, in the fall, the contents of old chests, boxes, drawers, and dark closets were brought forth to the light, a state of affairs truly frightful to a housekeeper, was presented. One of the breadths of my handsome carpet had the pile so eaten off in conspicuous places, that no remedy was left but the purchase and substitution of a new one, at a cost of nearly ten dollars. In dozens of places the texture of the carpet was eaten entirely through. I was, as my lady readers may naturally suppose, very unhappy at this. But, the evil by no means found a limit here. On opening my fur boxes, I found that the work of destruction had been going on there also. A single shake of the muff, threw little fibres and flakes of fur in no stinted measure upon the air; and, on dashing my hand hard against it, a larger mass was detached, showing the skin bare and white beneath. My furs were ruined. They had cost seventy dollars, and were not worth ten!

A still further examination into our stock of winter clothing, showed that the work of destruction had extended to almost every article. Scarcely any thing had escaped.

Troubled, worried, and unhappy as I was, I yet concealed from Mr. Smith the origin of all this ruin. He never suspected our cheap sofa for a moment. After I had, by slow degrees, recovered from my chagrin and disappointment, my thoughts turned, naturally, upon a disposition of the sofa. What was to be done with it? As to keeping it over another season, that was not to be thought of for a moment. But, would it be right, I asked myself, to send it back to auctions and let it thus go into the possession of some housekeeper, as ignorant of its real character as I had been? I found it very hard to reconcile my conscience to such a disposition of the sofa. And there was still another difficulty in the way. What excuse for parting with it could I make to Mr. Smith? He had never suspected that article to be the origination of all the mischief and loss we had sustained.

Winter began drawing to a close, and still the sofa remained in

T. S. Arthur

its place, and still was I in perplexity as to what should be done with it.

"Business requires me to go to Charleston," said Mr. Smith, one day late in February.

"How long will you be away?" was my natural enquiry.

"From ten days to two weeks," replied Mr. Smith.

"So long as that?"

"It will hardly be possible to get home earlier than the time I have mentioned."

"You go in the Osprey?"

"Yes. She sails day after to-morrow. So you will have all ready for me, if you please."

Never before had the announcement of my husband that he had to go away on business given me pleasure. The moment he said that he would be absent, the remedy for my difficulty suggested itself.

The very day Mr. Smith sailed in the steamer for Charleston, I sent for an upholsterer, and after explaining to him the defect connected with my sofa, directed him to have the seating all removed, and then replaced by new materials, taking particular care to thoroughly cleanse the inside of the wood work, lest the vestige of a moth should be left remaining.

All this was done, at a cost of twenty dollars. When Mr. Smith returned, the sofa was back in its place; and he was none the wiser for the change, until some months afterwards, when, unable to keep the secret any longer, I told him the whole story.

I am pretty well cured, I think now, of bargain-buying.

CHAPTER XXII

A PEEVISH DAY AND ITS CONSEQUENCES

THERE are few housekeepers who have not had their sick and peevish days. I have had mine, as the reader will see by the following story, which I some time since ventured to relate, in the third person, and which I now take the liberty of introducing into these confessions.

"It is too bad, Rachel, to put me to all this trouble; and you know I can hardly hold up my head."

Thus spoke Mrs. Smith, in a peevish voice, to a quiet looking domestic, who had been called up from the kitchen to supply some unimportant omission in the breakfast table arrangement.

Rachel looked hurt and rebuked, but made no reply.

"How could you speak in that way to Rachel?" said Mr. Smith, as soon as the domestic had withdrawn.

"If you felt just as I do, Mr. Smith, you would speak cross, too!" Mrs. Smith replied a little warmly - "I feel just like a rag; and my head aches as if it would burst."

"I know you feel badly, and I am very sorry for you. But still, I suppose it is as easy to speak kindly as harshly. Rachel is very obliging and attentive, and should be borne with in occasional omissions, which you of course know are not wilful."

"It is easy enough to preach," retorted Mrs. Smith, whose temper, from bodily lassitude and pain, was in quite an irritable state. The reader will understand at least one of the reasons of this, when he is told that the scene here presented occurred during the last oppressive week in August.

Mr. Smith said no more. He saw that to do so would only be to provoke instead of quieting his wife's ill humor. The morning meal went by in silence, but little food passing the lips of either. How could it, when the thermometer was ninety-four at eight o'clock in the morning, and the leaves upon the trees were as motionless as if suspended in a vacuum. Bodies and minds were relaxed - and the one turned from food, as the other did from thought, with an instinctive aversion.

After Mr. Smith had left his home for his place of business, Mrs. Smith went up into her chamber, and threw herself upon the bed, her head still continuing to ache with great violence. It so happened that a week before, the chambermaid had gone away, sick, and all the duties of the household had in consequence devolved upon Rachel, herself not very well. Cheerfully, however, had she endeavored to discharge these accumulated duties, and but for the unhappy, peevish state of mind in which Mrs. Smith indulged, would have discharged them without a murmuring thought. But, as she was a faithful, conscientious woman, and, withal, sensitive in her feelings, to be found fault with, worried her exceedingly. Of this Mrs. Smith was well aware, and had, until the latter part of the trying month of August, acted towards Rachel with consideration and forbearance. But the last week of August was too much for her. The sickness of the chamber maid threw such heavy duties upon Rachel, whose daily headaches and nervous relaxation of body were borne without a complaint, that their perfect performance was almost impossible. Slight omissions, which were next to unavoidable, under the circumstances, became so annoying to Mrs. Smith, herself, as it has been seen, laboring under great bodily and mental prostration that she could not bear them.

"She knows better, and she could do better, if she chose," was her rather uncharitable comment, often inwardly made on the occurrence of some new trouble.

After Mr. Smith had taken his departure on the morning just referred to, Mrs. Smith went up into her chamber, as has been seen, and threw herself languidly upon a bed, pressing her hands to her throbbing temples, as she did so, and murmuring:

"I can't live at this rate!"

At the same time, Rachel sat down in the kitchen the large waiter upon which she had arranged the dishes from the breakfast table, and then sinking into a chair, pressed one hand upon her forehead, and sat for more than a minute in troubled silence. It had been three days since she had received from Mrs. Smith a pleasant word, and the last remark, made to her a short time before, had been the unkindest of all. At another time, even all this would not have moved her - she could have perceived that Mrs. Smith was not in a right state - that lassitude of body had produced a temporary infirmity of mind. But, being herself affected by the oppressive season almost as much as her mistress, she could not make these allowances. While still seated, the chamber bell was rung with a quick, startling jerk.

"What next?" peevishly ejaculated Rachel, and then slowly proceeded to obey the summons.

"How could you leave my chamber in such a condition as this?" was the salutation that met her ear, as she entered the presence of Mrs. Smith, who, half raised upon the bed, and leaning upon her hand, looked the very personification of languor, peevishness, and ill-humor. "You had plenty of time while we were eating breakfast to have put things a little to rights!"

To this Rachel made no reply, but turned away and went back into the kitchen. She had scarcely reached that spot, before the bell rang again, louder and quicker than before; but she did not answer it. In about three minutes it was jerked with an energy that snapped the wire, but Rachel was immovable. Five minutes elapsed, and then Mrs. Smith fully aroused, from the lethargy that had stolen over her, came down with a quick, firm step.

"What's the reason you didn't answer my bell? say?" she asked, in an excited voice.

Rachel did not reply.

"Do you hear me?"

Rachel had never been so treated before; she had lived with Mrs. Smith, for three years, and had rarely been found fault with. She had been too strict in regard, to the performance of her duty to leave much room for even a more exacting mistress to find fault; but now, to be overtasked and sick, and to be chidden, rebuked, and even angrily assailed, was more than she could well bear. She did not suffer herself to speak for some moments, and then her voice trembled, and the tears came out upon her cheeks.

"I wish you to get another in my place. I find I don't suit you. My time will be up day after to-morrow."

"Very well," was Mrs. Smith's firm reply, as she turned away, and left the kitchen,

Here was trouble in good earnest. Often and often had Mrs. Smith said, during the past two or three years - "What should I do without Rachel?" And now she had given notice that she was going to leave her, and under circumstances which made pride forbid a request to stay. Determined to act out her part of the business with firmness and decision, she dressed herself and went out, hot and oppressive as it was, and took her way to an intelligence office, where she paid the required fee, and directed a cook and chamber maid to be sent to her. On the next morning, about ten o'clock, an Irish girl came and offered herself as a cook, and was, after sundry questions and answers, engaged. So soon as this negotiation was settled, Rachel retired from the kitchen, leaving the new-comer in full possession. In half an hour after she received her wages, and left, in no very happy frame of mind, a home that had been for three years, until within a few days, a pleasant one. As for Mrs. Smith, she was ready to go to bed sick; but this was impracticable. Nancy, the new cook, had expressly stipulated that she was to have no duties unconnected with the kitchen. The consequence was, that, notwithstanding the thermometer ranged above ninety, and the atmosphere remained as sultry as air from a heated oven, Mrs. Smith was compelled to arrange her chamber and parlors. By the time this was done she was in a condition to go to bed, and lie until dinner time. The arrival of this important period brought new troubles and vexations. Dinner was late by forty minutes, and then came on the table in a most abominable condition. A fine sirloin was burnt to a crisp. The tomatoes were smoked, and the potatoes watery. As if this were not enough to mar the pleasure of the dinner hour for a hungry husband, Mrs. Smith added thereto a distressed countenance and discouraging complaints. Nancy was grumbled at and scolded every time she had occasion to appear in the room, and her single attempt to excuse herself on account of not understanding the cook stove, was met by:

"Do hush, will you! I'm out of all patience!"

As to the latter part of the sentence, that was a needless waste of words. The condition of mind she described was fully apparent.

About three o'clock in the afternoon, just as Mrs. Smith had found a temporary relief from a troubled mind and a most intolerable headache, in sleep, a tap on the chamber door awoke her, there stood Nancy, all equipped for going out.

T. S. Arthur

"I find I won't suit you, ma'am," said Nancy, "and so you must look out for another girl."

Having said this, she turned away and took her departure, leaving Mrs. Smith in a state of mind, as it is said, "more easily imagined than described."

"O dear! what shall I do!" at length broke from her lips, as she burst into tears, and burying her face in the pillow, sobbed aloud. Already she had repented of her fretfulness and fault-finding temper, as displayed towards Rachel, and could she have made a truce with pride, or silenced its whispers, would have sent for her well-tried domestic, and endeavored to make all fair with her again. But, under the circumstances, this was now impossible. While yet undetermined how to act, the street bell rung, and she was compelled to attend the door, as she was now alone in the house. She found, on opening it, a rough-looking country girl, who asked if she were the lady who wanted a chamber maid. Any kind of help was better than none at all, and so Mrs. Smith asked the young woman to walk in. In treating with her in regard to her qualifications for the situation she applied for, she discovered that she knew "almost nothing at all about any thing." The stipulation that she was to be a doer-of-all-work-in-general, until a cook could be obtained, was readily agreed to, and then she was shown to her room in the attic, where she prepared herself for entering upon her duties.

"Will you please, ma'am, show me what you want me to do?" asked the new help, presenting herself before Mrs. Smith.

"Go into the kitchen, Ellen, and see that the fire is made. I'll be down there presently."

To be compelled to see after a new and ignorant servant, and direct her in every thing, just at, so trying a season of the year, and while her mind was "all out of sorts," was a severe task for poor Mrs. Smith. She found that Ellen, as she had too good reason for believing, was totally unacquainted with kitchen work. She did not even know how to kindle a coal fire; nor could she manage the stove after Mrs. Smith had made the fire for her. All this did not in any way tend to make her less unhappy or more patient than before. On retiring for the night, she had a high fever, which continued unabated until morning, when her husband found her really ill; so much so as to make the attendance of a doctor necessary.

A change in the air had taken place during the night, and the temperature had fallen many degrees. This aided the efforts of the physician, and enabled him so to adapt his remedies as to speedily break the fever. But the ignorance and awkwardness of Ellen, apparent in her attempts to arrange her bed and chamber, so worried her mind, that she was near relapsing into her former feverish and excited state. The attendance of an elder maiden sister was just in time. All care was taken from her thoughts, and she had a chance of recovering a more healthy tone of mind and body. During the next week, she knew little or nothing of how matters were progressing out of her own chamber. A new cook had been hired, of whom she was pleased to hear good accounts, although she had not seen her, and Ellen, under the mild and judicious instruction of her sister, had learned to make up a bed neatly, to sweep, and dust in true style, and to perform all the little etceteras of chamber-work greatly to her satisfaction. She was, likewise, good tempered, willing, and to all appearances strictly trust-worthy.

One morning, about a week after she had become too ill to keep up, she found herself so far recovered as to be able to go down stairs to breakfast. Every thing upon the table she found arranged in the neatest style. The food was well cooked, especially some tender rice cakes, of which she was very fond.

"Really, these are delicious!" said she, as the finely flavored cakes almost melted in her mouth. "And this coffee is just the thing! How fortunate we have been to obtain so good a cook! I was afraid we should never be able to replace Rachel. But even she is equalled, if not surpassed."

T. S. Arthur

"Still she does not surpass Rachel," said Mr. Smith, a little gravely. "Rachel was a treasure."

"Indeed she was. And I have been sorry enough I ever let her go," returned Mrs. Smith.

At that moment a new cook entered with a plate of warm cakes.

"Rachel!" ejaculated Mrs. Smith, letting her knife and fork fall. "How do you do? I am glad to see you! Welcome home again!"

As she spoke quickly and earnestly, she held out her hand, and grasped that of her old domestic warmly. Rachel could not speak, but as she left the room she put her apron to her eyes. (sic) Her's were not the only ones dim with rising moisture.

For at least a year to come, both Mrs. Smith and her excellent cook will have no cause to complain of each other. How they will get along during the last week of next August, we cannot say, but hope the lesson they have both received will teach them to bear and forbear.

CHAPTER XXIII

WORDS

"THE foolish thing!" said my aunt Rachel, speaking warmly, "to get hurt at a mere word. It's a little hard that people can't open their lips but somebody is offended."

"Words are things!" said I, smiling.

"Very light things! A person must be tender, indeed, that is hurt by a word."

"The very lightest thing may hurt, if it falls on a tender place."

"I don't like people who have these tender places," said aunt Rachel. "I never get hurt at what is said to me. No - never! To be ever picking and mincing, and chopping off your words - to be afraid to say this or that - for fear somebody will be offended! I can't abide it!"

"People who have these tender places can't help it, I suppose. This being so, ought we not to regard their weakness?" said I. "Pain, either of body or mind, is hard to bear, and we should not inflict it causelessly."

"People who are so wonderfully sensitive," replied aunt Rachel, growing warmer, "ought to shut themselves up at home, and not come among sensible, good tempered persons. As far as I am concerned, I can tell them, one and all, that I am not going to pick out every hard word from a sentence as carefully as I would seeds from a raisin. Let them crack them with their teeth, if they are afraid to swallow them whole."

Now, for all that aunt Rachel went on after this strain, she was a kind, good soul, in the main, and I could see, was sorry for having hurt the feelings of Mary Lane. But she didn't like to acknowledge that she was in the wrong; that would detract too much from the self-complacency with which she regarded herself. Knowing her character very well, I thought it best not to continue the little argument about the importance of words, and so changed the subject. But, every now and then, aunt Rachel would return to it, each time softening a little towards Mary. At last she said:

"I'm sure it was a little thing. A very little thing. She might have known that nothing unkind was intended on my part."

"There are some subjects, aunt," I replied, "to which we cannot bear the slightest allusion. And a sudden reference to them is very apt to throw us off of our guard. What you said to Mary, has, in all probability, touched some weakness of character, or probed some wound that time has been able to heal. I have always thought her a sensible, good natured girl."

"And so have I. But I really cannot think that she has shown her good sense or good nature in the present case. It is a very bad failing this, of being over sensitive; and exceedingly annoying to one's friends."

"It is, I know; but still, all of us have a weak point, and when that is assailed, we are very apt to betray our feelings."

"Well, I say now, as I have always said - I don't like to have any thing to do with people who have these weak points. This being hurt by a word, as if words were blows, is something that does not come within the range of my sympathies."

"And yet, aunt," said I, "all have weak points. Even you are not entirely free from them."

"Me!" aunt Rachel bridled.

"Yes; and if even as light a thing as a word were to fall upon them, you would suffer pain."

"Pray, ma'am," said, aunt Rachel, with much dignity of manner; she was chafed by my words, light as they were; "inform me where these weaknesses, of which you are pleased to speak, lie?"

"Oh, no; you must excuse me. That would be very much out of place. But I only stated a general fact that appertains to all of us."

Aunt Rachel looked very grave. I had laid the weight of words upon a weakness of her character, and it had given her pain. That weakness was a peculiarly good opinion of herself. I had made no allegation against her; and there was none in my mind. My words simply expressed the general truth that we all have weaknesses, and included her in their application. But she imagined that I referred to some particular defect or fault, and mail-proof as she was against words, they had wounded her.

For a day or two, aunt Rachel remained more sober than was her wont. I knew the cause, but did not attempt to remove from her mind an impression my words had made. One day, about a week after, I said to her:

"Aunt Rachel, I saw Mary Lane's mother this morning."

"Ah?" The old lady looked up at me enquiringly.

"I don't wonder your words hurt the poor girl," I added.

"Why? What did I say?" quickly asked aunt Rachel.

"You said that she was a jilt."

T. S. Arthur

"But I was only in jest, and she knew it. I did not really mean any thing. I'm surprised that Mary should be so foolish."

"You will not be surprised when you know all," was my answer.

"All? What all? I'm sure I wasn't in earnest. I didn't mean to hurt the poor girl's feelings."

My aunt looked very much troubled.

"No one blames you, aunt Rachel," said I. "Mary knows you didn't intend wounding her."

"But why should she take a little word so much to heart? It must have had more truth in it than I supposed."

"Did you know that Mary refused an offer of marriage from Walter Green, last week?"

"Why, no! It can't be possible! Refused Walter Green?"

"Yes."

"They've been intimate for a long time."

"I know."

"She certainly encouraged him."

"I think it more than probable."

"Is it possible, then, that she did really jilt the young man?" exclaimed aunt Rachel.

"This has been said of her," I replied. "But, as far as I can learn, she was really attached to him, and suffered great pain in rejecting his offer. Wisely she regarded marriage as the most important event of her life, and refused to make so solemn a contract with one in whose principles she had not the fullest confidence."

"But she ought not to have encouraged Walter, if she did not intend marrying him," said aunt Rachel, with some warmth.

"She encouraged him so long as she thought well of him. A closer view revealed points of character hidden by distance. When she saw these, her feelings were already deeply involved. But, like a true woman, she turned from the proffered hand, even though, while in doing so, her heart palpitated with pain. There is nothing false about Mary Lane. She could no more trifle with a lover than she could commit a crime. Think, then, how almost impossible it would be for her to hear herself called, under existing circumstances, even in sport, a jilt, without being hurt. Words sometimes have power to hurt more than blows. Do you not see this now, aunt Rachel?"

"Oh, yes, yes. I see it; and I saw it before," said the old lady. "And, in future, I will be more careful of my words. It is pretty late in life to learn this lesson - but we are never too late to learn. Poor Mary! It grieves me to think that I should have hurt her so much."

Yes, words often have in them a smarting force, and we cannot be too guarded how we use them. "Think twice before you speak once," is a trite, but wise saying. We teach it to our children very carefully, but are too apt to forget that it has not lost its application to ourselves.

CHAPTER XXIV

MAY BE SO

"NEXT time you go out, you'll buy me a wagon, won't you, mother?"said my little boy to me, one day.

I didn't want to say "no," and destroy his happy feelings; and I was not prepared to say "yes;" and so I gave the evasive reply so often used under such circumstances, "May be so," and which was meant rather as a negative than an affirmative. The child was satisfied; for he gave my words the meaning he wished them to have. In a little while after, I had forgotten all about it. Not so my boy. To him the "May be so" was "yes," and he set his heart, confidently, on receiving the wagon the next time I should go out. This happened on the afternoon of that very day. It was towards evening when I returned. The moment I rung the bell at my own door, I heard his pattering feet and gleeful voice in the entry.

"Where's my wagon?" said he, as I entered, a shade of disappointment falling suddenly upon his excited, happy face.

"What wagon, dear?" I asked.

"My wagon. The wagon you promised to buy me."

"I didn't promise to buy a wagon, my son."

"Oh, yes you did, mother! You promised me this morning."

Tears were already in his eye, and his face wore a look of distressing disappointment.

"I promised to buy you a wagon? I am sure I remember nothing about it," I replied confidently. "What in the world put that into your head?"

"Didn't I ask you?" said the child, the tears now overflowing his cheeks.

"Yes, I believe you did ask me something about a wagon; but I didn't promise to buy you one."

"Oh, yes you did, mother. You said may be so."

"But 'may be so' doesn't mean yes."

At this the little fellow uttered a distressing cry. His heart was almost broken by disappointment. He had interpreted my words according to his own wishes, and not according to their real meaning.

Unprepared for an occurrence of this kind, I was not in the mood to sympathise with my child fully. To be met thus, at the moment of my return home, disturbed me.

"I didn't promise to buy you a wagon; and you must stop crying about it," said I, seeing that he had given way to his feelings, and was crying in a loud voice.

But he cried on. I went up stairs to lay off my things, and he followed, still crying.

"You must hush, now," said I, more positively. "I cannot permit this. I never promised to buy you a wagon."

"You said may be so," sobbed the child.

"May be so, and yes, are two different things. If I had said that

I would buy you a wagon, then there would have been some reason in your disappointment; but I said no such thing."

He had paused to listen; but, as I ceased speaking, his crying was renewed.

"You must stop this now. There is no use in it, and I will not have it," said I, resolutely.

My boy choked down for a few moments at this, and half stifled his grief; but o'ermastering him, it flowed on again as wildly as ever. I felt impatient.

"Stop this moment, I say!" And I took hold of his arm firmly. My will is strong, and when a little excited, it often leads me beyond where I would go in moments of reflection. My boy knew this by experience. By my manner of speaking he saw that I was in earnest, and that, if he did not obey me, punishment would follow. So, with what must have been a powerful effort for one so young, he stifled the utterance of his grief. But, the storm within raged none the less violently, and I could see his little frame quiver as he strove to repress the rising sobs.

Turning away from me, he went and sat down on a low seat in a corner of the room. I saw his form in the glass as I stood before it to arrange my hair, after laying aside my bonnet; and for the first time my feelings were touched. There was an abandonment in his whole attitude; an air of grief about him that affected me with pity and tenderness.

"Poor child!" I sighed. "His heart is almost broken. I ought to have said yes or no; and then all would have been settled."

"Come," said I, after a few moments, reaching my hand towards the child - "let us go down and look out for father. He will be home soon."

I spoke kindly and cheerfully. But he neither moved, looked

up, nor gave the smallest sign that he heard me.

"Oh, well," said I, with some impatience in my voice - "it doesn't matter at all. If you'd rather sit there than come down into the parlor and look out for dear father, you can please yourself."

And turning away as I spoke, I left the chamber, and went down stairs. Seating myself at the window, I looked forth and endeavored to feel unconcerned and cheerful. But, this was beyond my power. I saw nothing but the form of my grieving child, and could think of nothing but his sorrow and disappointment.

"Nancy," said I to one of my domestics, who happened to come into the parlor to ask me some question, "I wish you would run down to the toy store in the next block, and buy Neddy a wagon. His heart is almost broken about one."

The girl, always willing, when kindly spoke to, ran off to obey my wishes, and in a little while came back with the article wanted.

"Now," said I, "go up into my room and tell Neddy that I've got something for him. Don't mention the wagon; I want to take him by surprise."

Nancy went bounding up the stairs, and I placed the wagon in the centre of the room where it would meet the child's eyes on the moment of his entrance, and then sat down to await his coming, and enjoy his surprise and delight.

After the lapse of about a minute, I heard Nancy coming down slowly.

"Neddy's asleep," said she, looking in at the door.

"Asleep!" I felt greatly disappointed.

"Yes, ma'am. He was on the floor asleep. I took him up, and laid him in your bed."

"Then he's over his troubles," said I, attempting to find a relief for my feelings in this utterance. But no such relief came.

Taking the wagon in my hand, I went up to the chamber where he lay, and bent over him. The signs of grief were still upon his innocent face, and every now and then a faint sigh or sob gave evidence that even sleep had not yet hushed entirely, the storm which had swept over him.

"Neddy!" I spoke to him in a voice of tenderness, hoping that my words might reach his ear, "Neddy, dear, I've bought you a wagon."

But his senses were locked. Taking him up, I undressed him, and then, after kissing his lips, brow, and cheeks, laid him in his little bed, and placed the wagon on the pillow beside him.

Even until the late hour at which I retired on that evening, were my feelings oppressed by the incident I have described. My "May be so," uttered in order to avoid giving the direct answer my child wanted, had occasioned him far more pain than a positive refusal of his request could have done.

"I will be more careful in future," said I, as I lay thinking about the occurrence, "how I create false hopes. My yea shall be yea, and my nay nay. Of these cometh not evil."

In the morning when I awoke, I found Neddy in possession of his wagon. He was running with it around the room, as happy as if a tear had never been upon his cheek. I looked at him for many minutes without speaking. At last, seeing that I was awake, he bounded up to the bedside, and, kissing me, said:

"Thank you, dear mother, for buying me this wagon! You are a good mother!"

I must own to having felt some doubts on the subject of Neddy's compliment at the time. Since this little experience, I have been more careful how I answer the petitions of my children; and avoid the "May be so," "I'll see about it," and other such evasive answers that come so readily to the lips. The good result I have experienced in many instances.

CHAPTER XXV

"THE POOR CHILD DIED"

MY baby, nine months old, had some fever, and seemed very unwell. One neighbor said:

"You'd better send for the doctor."

Another suggested that it had, no doubt, eaten something that disagreed with it, and that a little antimonial wine would enable it to throw it off; another advised a few grains of calomel, and another a dose of rheubarb. But I said:

"No. I'll wait a little while, and see if it won't get better."

"You should give him medicine in time. Many a person dies from not taking medicine in time;" said a lady who expressed more than usual concern for the well-being of my baby. She had a very sick child herself.

"Many more die," I replied, "from taking medicine too soon. I believe that one half of the diseases in the world are produced by medicines, and that the other half are often made worse by their injudicious administration."

"You'd better send for the doctor," urged the lady.

"No. I'll wait until the morning, and then, if he's no better, or should be worse, I'll call in our physician. Children often appear very sick one hour, and are comparatively well again in the next."

"It's a great risk," said the lady, gravely. "A very great risk. I called in the doctor the moment my dear little Eddy began to droop about. And it's well I did. He's near death's door as it is; and without medical aid I would certainly have lost him before this. He's only been sick a week, and you know yourself how low he is reduced. Where do you think he would have been without medicine? The disease has taken a terrible hold of him. Why, the doctor has bled him twice; and his little chest is raw all over from a blister. He has been cupped and leeched. We have had mustard plasters upon his arms and the calves of his legs. I don't know how many grains of calomel he has taken; and it has salivated him dreadfully. Oh! such a sore mouth! Poor child! He suffers dreadfully. Besides, he has taken some kind of powder almost every hour. They are dreadfully nauseous; and we have to hold him, every time, and pour them down his throat. Oh, dear! It makes my heart sick. Now, with all this, the disease hangs on almost as bad as ever. Suppose we hadn't sent for the doctor at first? Can't you see what would have been the consequence? It is very wrong to put off calling in a physician upon the first symptoms of a disease."

"Pardon me, Mrs. Lee, for saying so," was my reply, "but I cannot help thinking that, if you had not called the doctor, your child would have been quite well to-day."

Mrs. Lee - that was the lady's name - uttered an exclamation of surprise and disapproval of my remark.

"But, cannot you see, yourself; that it is not the disease that has reduced your child so low. The bleeding, blistering, cupping, leeching, and calomel administrations, would have done all this, had your child been perfectly well when it went into the doctor's hands."

"But the disease would have killed him inevitably. If it requires all this to break it, don't you see that it must have taken a most fatal hold on the poor child's system."

"No, Mrs. Lee, I cannot see any such thing," was my reply. "The medicine probably fixed the disease, that would, if left alone, have retired of itself. What does the doctor say ails the child?"

"He does not seem to know. There seems to be a complication of diseases."

"Produced by the treatment, no doubt. If there had been scarlet fever, or small pox, or croup, active and energetic treatment would, probably, have been required, and the doctor would have known what he was about in administering his remedies. But, in a slight indisposition, like that from which your child suffered, it is, in my opinion, always better to give no medicine for a time. Drugs thrown into the tender system of a child, will always produce disease of some kind, more or less severe; and where slight disorders already exist, they are apt to give them a dangerous hold upon the body, or, uniting with them, cause a most serious, and, at times, fatal illness."

But Mrs. Lee shook her head. She thought the doctors knew best. They had great confidence in their family physician. He had doctored them through many dangerous attacks, and had always brought them through safely. As to the new-fangled notions about giving little or no medicine, she had no confidence in them. Medicine was necessary at times, and she always gave her children medicine at least two, or three times a year, whether they were sick or well. Prevention, in her eyes, was better than cure. And where there was actual sickness, she was in favor of vigorous treatment. One good dose of medicine would do more good than a hundred little ones; with much more to the same effect.

On the next morning, my dear baby, who was just as sick for a few hours as Mrs. Lee's child was at first, was as well as ever.

Not long after breakfast, I was sent for by Mrs. Lee. Her poor child was much worse. The servant said that she was sure it was dying. I changed my dress hurriedly, and went over to the house of my neighbor.

Shall I describe the painful object that met my sight? It was three days since I had seen the little sufferer; but, oh! how it had changed in that brief time. Its face was sunken, its eyes far back in their sockets, and its forehead marked with lines of suffering. The whole of its breast was raw from the blister, and its mouth, lying open, showed, with painful distinctness, the dreadful injury wrought by the mercury thrown, with such a liberal hand, into its delicate system. All the life seemed to have withdrawn itself from the skin; for the vital forces, in the centre of its body, were acting but feebly.

The doctor came in while I was there. He said but little. It was plain that he was entirely at fault, and that he saw no hope of a favorable issue. All his, "active treatment" had tended to break down the child, rather than cure the disease from which it at first suffered. There was a great deal of heat about the child's head, and he said something about having it shaved for a blister.

"Wouldn't ice do better, doctor?" I felt constrained to suggest. He turned upon me quickly and seemed annoyed.

"No, madam!" he replied with dignity.

I said no more, for I felt how vain my words would be. The blister, however, was not ordered; but, in its stead, mustard plasters were directed to be placed over the feet and legs to the knees, and a solution of iodine, or iron, I don't now remember which, prescribed, to be given every half hour.

I went home, some time after the doctor left, feeling sick at heart. "They are murdering that child," I could not help saying to myself. My own dear babe I found full of health and life; and I hugged it to my breast with a feeling of thankfulness.

T. S. Arthur

Before the day closed, Mrs. Lee's poor child died. Was it a cause of wonder?

CHAPTER XXVI

THE RIVAL BONNETS

I HAVE a pleasant story to relate of a couple of fashionables of our city, which will serve to diversify these "Confessions," and amuse the reader. To the incidents, true in the main, I have taken the liberty of adding some slight variations of my own.

A lady of some note in society, named Mrs. Claudine, received a very beautiful bonnet from New York, a little in advance of others, and being one of the rival leaders in the fashionable world, felt some self-complacency at the thought of appearing abroad in the elegant head-gear, and thereby getting the reputation of leading the fashion.

Notwithstanding Mrs. Claudine's efforts to keep the matter a secret, and thus be able to create a surprise when she appeared at church on the next Sunday, the fact that she had received the bonnet leaked out, and there was some excitement about it. Among those who heard of the new bonnet, was a Mrs. Ballman, who had written to a friend to get for her the very article obtained first by Mrs. Claudine. From some cause or other a delay had occurred, and to her chagrin she learned that a rival had the new fashion, and would get the *eclat* that she so much coveted. The disappointment, to one whose pleasures in life are so circumscribed as those of a real fashionable lady, was severe indeed. She did not sleep more than a few hours on the night after she received the mortifying intelligence.

T. S. Arthur

The year before, Mrs. Claudine had led the fashion in some article of dress, and to see her carry off the palm in bonnets on this occasion, when she had striven so hard to be in advance, was more than Mrs. Bellman could endure. The result of a night's thinking on the subject was a determination to pursue a very extraordinary course, the nature of which will be seen. By telegraph Mrs. Bellman communicated with her friend in New York, desiring her to send on by the evening of the next day, which was Saturday, the bonnet she had ordered, if four prices had to be paid as an inducement to get the milliner to use extra exertions in getting it up. In due time, notice came back that the bonnet would be sent on by express on Saturday, much to the joy of Mrs. Ballman, who from the interest she felt in carrying out her intentions, had entirely recovered from the painful disappointment at first experienced.

Saturday brought the bonnet, and a beautiful one it was. A few natural sighs were expended over the elegant affair, and then other feelings came in to chase away regrets at not having been first to secure the article.

On the day previous, Friday, Mrs. Ballman called upon a fashionable milliner, and held with her the following conversation.

"You have heard of Mrs. Claudine's new bonnet, I presume?"

"Yes, madam," replied the milliner.

"Do you think it will take?" asked Mrs. Ballman.

"I do."

"You have not the pattern?"

"Oh, yes. I received one a week ago."

"You did!"

"Yes. But some one must introduce it. As Mrs. Claudine is about doing this there is little doubt of its becoming the fashion, for the style is striking as well as tasteful."

Mrs. Ballman mused for some moments. There she drew the milliner aside, and said, in a low confidential tone.

"Do you think you could get up a bonnet a handsome as that, and in just as good taste?"

"I know I could. In my last received London and Paris fashions are several bonnets a handsome as the one that is about being adopted in New York, and here also without doubt."

"I am not so sure of its being adopted here," said the lady.

"If Mrs. Claudine introduces it, as I understand she intends doing on Sunday, it will certainly be approved and the style followed."

"I very much doubt it. But we will see. Where are the bonnets you spoke of just now?"

The milliner brought forth a number of pattern cards and plates, and pointed out two bonnets, either of which, in her judgment, was more beautiful than the one Mrs. Claudine had received.

"Far handsomer," was the brief remark with which Mrs. Ballman approved the milliner's judgment. "And now," she added, "can you get me up one of these by Sunday?"

"I will try."

"Try won't do," said the lady, with some excitement in her manner. "I must have the bonnet. Can you make it?"

"Yes."

"Very well. Then make it. And let it be done in your very best manner. Why I wish to have this bonnet I need hardly explain to you. I believed that I would have received the bonnet, about to be adopted in New York, first. I had written to a friend to procure it; but, by some means, Mrs. Claudine has obtained (sic) her's in advance of me. Mine will be here to-morrow, but I don't mean to wear it. I wish to lead."

"If you were both to appear in this bonnet, the fashion would be decided," said the milliner.

"I know. But I have no wish to share the honor with Mrs. Claudine. Make me the bonnet I have selected, and I will see that it puts (sic) her's down."

"You will remember," said the milliner, "that (sic) her's has been already adopted in New York. This will be almost sure to give it the preference. It would be better that you did not attempt a rivalry, than that you should be beaten."

"But I don't mean to be beaten," replied the lady. "I have taken measures to prevent that. After Sunday you will hear no more of the New York bonnet. Mine will go, and this, I need not tell you, will be a feather in your cap, and dollars in your pocket; as I will refer to you as the only one who can get it up. So do your best, and improve the pattern we have selected, if it will bear improvement."

The milliner promised to do her "prettiest," and Mrs. Ballman returned home in a state of considerable elation at the prospect of carrying off the palm, and humiliating her rival at the same time.

Mrs. Claudine, though a little vain, and fond of excelling, was a woman of kind feelings, and entirely superior to the petty jealousies that annoyed Mrs. Ballman, and soured her towards all who succeeded in rivalling her in matters of taste and fashion. Of what was passing in the mind of the lady who had been so troubled at her reception of a new style of bonnet from

New York, she was entirely ignorant. She was not even aware that Mrs. Ballman had ordered the same article, nor that she had suffered a disappointment.

Saturday came. Mrs. Claudine was busy over some little article of dress that was to add to her appearance on the next day, when an Irish girl, who had formerly lived with her, entered her room.

"Ah! Kitty!" said the lady pleasantly. "How do you do?"

"I'm right well, mum, thankee," replied Kitty, with a courtesy.

"Where do you live now, Kitty?" inquired Mrs. Claudine.

"I'm living with Mrs. Ballman," said the girl.

"A very good place, I have no doubt."

"Oh, yes, mum. It is a good place. I hain't much to do, barrin' going out with the children on good days, and seein' after them in the house; and I get good wages."

"I'm very glad to hear it, Kitty; and hope you will not give up so good a home."

"No, indeed, mum; and I won't do that. But Mrs. Claudine - "

Kitty's face flushed, and she stammered in her speech.

"What do you wish to say?" inquired the lady, seeing that Kitty hesitated to speak of what was on her mind.

"Indade, mum," said Kitty, evincing much perplexity, "I hardly know what I ought to do. But yez were good to me, mum, when I was sick and didn't send me off to the poor house like some girls are sent; and I never can forget yez while there's breath in me body. And now I've come to ask yez, just as a favor to me, not to wear that new bonnet from New

T. S. Arthur

York, to-morrow."

It was some moments before, the surprise occasioned by so novel and unexpected a request left Mrs. Claudine free to make any reply.

"Why, Kitty!" she at length exclaimed, "what on earth can you mean?"

"Indade, mum, and yez mustn't ask me what I mane, only don't wear the bonnet to church on the morrow, because - because - och, indade, mum, dear! I can't say any more. It wouldn't be right."

Mrs. Claudine told Kitty to sit down, an invitation which the girl, who was much agitated, accepted. The lady then remained silent and thoughtful for some time.

"Kitty," she remarked, at length, in a serious manner, "what you have said to me sounds very strangely. How you should know that I intended appearing in a new bonnet to-morrow, or why you should be so much interested in the matter is more than I can understand. As to acting as you desire, I see no reason for that whatever."

This reply only had the effect of causing Kitty to urge her request more strenuously. But she would give no reason for her singular conduct. After the girl had gone away, Mrs. Claudine laid aside her work - for she was not in a state of mind to do any thing but think - -and sat for at least an hour, musing upon the strange incident which had occurred. All at once, it flashed upon her mind that there must be some plot in progress to discredit or rival her new bonnet, which Kitty had learned at Mrs. Ballman's. The more she thought of this, the more fully did she become satisfied that it must be so. She was aware that Mrs. Ballman had been chagrined at her leading off in new fashions once or twice before; and the fact, evident now, that she knew of her reception of the bonnet, and Kitty's anxiety that she should not wear it on Sunday, led her to the conviction that there was some plot against her. At first, she determined to appear in her new bonnet, disregardful of Kitty's warning. But subsequent reflection brought her to a different conclusion.

The moment Mrs. Claudine settled it in her mind that she would not appear in the new bonnet, she began dressing herself, hurriedly, to go out. It was as late as five o'clock in the afternoon when she called at the store of the milliner who had been commissioned by Mrs. Ballman to get the rival bonnet.

"Have you the last fashions from abroad?" enquired Mrs. Claudine.

"We have," replied the milliner.

"Will you let me see them?"

"Certainly, ma'am."

And the patterns were shown. After examining them carefully, for some time, Mrs. Claudine selected a style of bonnet that pleased her fancy, and said -

"You must get me up this bonnet so that I can wear it to-morrow."

"Impossible, madam!" replied the milliner. "This is Saturday evening."

"I know it is; but for money you can get one of your girls to work all night. I don't care what you charge; but I must have the bonnet."

The milliner still hesitated, and seemed to be confused and uneasy. She asked Mrs. Claudine to sit down and wait for a little while, and then retired to think upon what she had better do. The fact was, Mrs. Claudine had pitched upon the very bonnet Mrs. Ballman had ordered, and her earnestness about

T. S. Arthur

having it made in time to wear on the next day, put it almost beyond her power to say no. If she were to tell her that Mrs. Ballman had ordered the same bonnet, it would, she knew, settle the matter. But, it occurred to her, that if both the ladies were to appear at church in the same style of bonnet, the fashion would be sure to take, and she, in consequence, get a large run of business. This thought sent the blood bounding through the milliner's veins, and decided her to keep her own counsel, and take Mrs. Claudine's order.

"She's as much right to the bonnet as Mrs. Ballman," settled all ethical questions that intruded themselves upon the milliner.

"I will have it ready for you," she said, on returning to Mrs. Claudine.

"Very well. But mind," said the lady, "I wish it got up in the very best style. The hurry must not take from its beauty. As for the price, charge what you please."

The milliner promised every thing, and Mrs. Claudine went home to think about the important events of the approaching Sabbath. On Sunday morning both bonnets were sent home, and both the ladies fully approved the style, effect, and all things appertaining to the elegant affairs.

At ten o'clock, Kitty, who was a broad-faced, coarse-looking Irish girl, came into the chamber of Mrs. Ballman, dressed up in her best, which was not saying much for the taste and elegance of her appearance.

"Are you all ready?" asked her mistress.

"Yes, mum."

"Very well, Kitty, here's the bonnet. Now, remember, you are to go into the pew just in front of ours. The Armburner's are all out of town, and there will be no one to occupy it."

Kitty received the elegant bonnet which had come on express from New York, and placed it upon her head.

"You really look charming," said the lady.

But Kitty was not flattered by her words, and evinced so little heart in what she was doing that Mrs Ballman said to her, in a half threatening tone, as she left the room -

"Mind, Kitty, I shall expect to see you at church."

"Oh, yes, mum; I'll be there," replied Kitty, courtesying awkwardly, and retiring.

Not long after Kitty had retired, Mrs. Ballman, after surveying, for many minutes, the effect of her new bonnet, becoming more and more pleased with it every moment, and more and more satisfied that it would "take," left her room, and was descending the stairs for the purpose of joining the family, who were awaiting her below. Just at that unlucky moment, a servant, who was bringing down a vessel of water, slipped, and a portion of the contents came dashing over the head and shoulders of the richly attired lady, ruining her elegant bonnet, and completely destroying the happy frame of mind in which she was about attending public worship. No wonder that she cried aloud from the sudden shock and distress so untoward an event occasioned; nor that she went back weeping to her chamber, and refused to be comforted.

Mr. Ballman and the children proceeded alone to church on that day. On their return home they found the lady in a calmer frame of mind. But Mr. Ballman looked grave and was unusually silent. Kitty came home and gave up her elegant head-dress; and when her mistress told her that she might keep it, she thanked her, but declined the present.

"You went to church, of course," she said.

"Oh, yes, mum," replied Kitty.

T. S. Arthur

"And sat in the Armburner's pew?"

"Yes, mum."

"Alone."

"Yes, mum."

"Was Mrs. Claudine there?"

"Yes, mum."

"Did she wear her new bonnet?"

"Yes, mum."

"It was exactly like this?"

"Oh, no, mum, it was exactly like the new one you had sent home this morning."

"What!" The face of the lady flushed instantly. "Wasn't it like this?"

"No, mum."

Mrs. Ballman sunk into a chair.

"You can retire, Kitty," she said, and the girl withdrew, leaving her to her own feelings and reflections, which were not of the most pleasing character.

The appearance of Kitty at church, fully explained to Mrs. Claudine the ungenerous game that had been played against her. Her first thought was to retaliate. But reflection brought other and better feelings into play. Instead of exposing what had been done, she destroyed the bonnet received from New York, and made an effort to keep what had occurred a secret. But Kitty's appearance at church in such an elegant affair, naturally created some talk. One surmise after another was started, and, at last, from hints dropped by the milliner, and admissions almost extorted from Mrs. Claudine, the truth came out so fully, that all understood it; nor was Mrs. Ballman long left in ignorance on this head.

As to the fashion, Mrs. Claudine's bonnet became the rage; though, as might be supposed, Mrs. Ballman refused to adopt it.

Who will be the successful rival next season, I am unable to predict. But it is believed that Mrs. Claudine intends giving Mrs. Ballman an advance of two weeks, and then coming in with a different style, and beating her in spite of the advantage.

T. S. Arthur

CHAPTER XXVII

MY WASHERWOMAN

WE were sitting at tea one evening - Mr. Smith, my sister and her husband, Mr. John Jones, and myself. In the midst of a pleasant conversation, Bridget looked into the dining-room.

"What is wanted?" said I.

"Mary Green is down stairs."

"Oh! the washerwoman."

"Yes ma'am."

"Well, what does she want?"

I knew what she wanted well enough. She had come for two dollars that I owed her. I felt annoyed. "Why?" the reader asks. "Obligations of this kind should always be met promptly and cheerfully."

True; and I am of those who never grudge the humble poor the reward of their labor. But, it so happened that I had received a pretty liberal supply of money from my husband on this very day, all of which I had spent in shopping. Some of my purchases could not be classed exactly under the head, "Articles of Domestic Economy," and I was, already, in rather a repentant mood - the warmth of admiration at the sight of sundry ornamental trifles having subsided almost as soon as I found myself their owner. To my question, Bridget very promptly answered,

"She's come for her money."

When a woman feels annoyed, she is rarely able to repress its exhibition. Men are cooler, and have a quicker self control. They make better hypocrites.

"She's very prompt," I remarked, a little fretfully, as I took out my porte-monnaie. Now I did not possess twenty cents, and I knew it; still, I fingered among its compartments as if in search of the little gold dollars that were not there.

"Hav'nt you the change?" enquired Mr. Smith, at the same time drawing forth his purse, through the meshes of which the gold and silver coin glittered in the gas light.

"No dear," I replied, feeling instant relief.

"Help yourself;" said he, as he tossed the purse to my side of the table. I was not long in accepting the invitation you may be sure.

"Dont think," said I, after Bridget had retired, "that I am one of those who grudge the toiling poor the meagre wages they earn. I presume I looked, as I spoke, a little annoyed. The fact is, to tell the honest truth, I have not a dollar in my porte-monnaie; this with the not very pleasant consciousness of having spent several dollars to-day rather foolishly, fretted me when the just demand of the washerwoman came."

"I will exonerate my wife from any suspicion of grinding the faces of the poor." Mr. Smith spoke promptly and with some earnestness of manner. After a slight pause, he continued,

"Some people have a singular reluctance to part with money. If waited on for a bill, they say, almost involuntarily, 'Call

T. S. Arthur

to-morrow,' even though their pockets are far from being empty.

"I once fell into this bad habit myself; but, a little incident, which I will relate, cured me. Not many years after I had attained my majority, a poor widow named Blake did my washing and ironing. She was the mother of two or three little children, whose sole dependance for food and raiment was on the labor of her hands.

"Punctually, every Thursday morning, Mrs. Blake appeared with my clothes, 'white as the driven snow;' but, not always, as punctually, did I pay the pittance she had earned by hard labor.

"'Mrs. Blake is down stairs,' said a servant tapping at my room door, one morning, while I was in the act of dressing myself.

"'Oh, very well,' I replied. 'Tell her to leave my clothes. I will get them when I come down.'

"The thought of paying the seventy-five cents, her due, crossed my mind. But, I said to myself, 'It's but a small matter, and will do as well when she comes again.'

"There was in this a certain reluctance to part with money. My funds were low, and I might need what change I had during the day. And so it proved! As I went to the office in which I was engaged, some small article of ornament caught my eye in a shop window.

"'Beautiful!' said I, as I stood looking at it. Admiration quickly changed into the desire for possession; and so I stepped in to ask the price. It was just two dollars.

"'Cheap enough,' thought I. And this very cheapness was a further temptation.

"So I turned out the contents of my pockets, counted them

over, and found the amount to be two dollars and a quarter.

"'I guess I'll take it,' said I, laying the money on the shop-keeper's counter.

"'Better have paid Mrs. Blake.' This thought crossed my mind, an hour afterwards, by which time, the little ornament had lost its power of pleasing. 'So much would at least have been saved.'

"I was leaving the table, after tea, on the evening that followed, when the waiter said to me -

"'Mrs. Blake is at the door, and wishes to see you.'

"I felt worried at hearing this; for there was no change in my pockets, and the poor washerwoman, had, of course, come for her money.

"'She's in a great hurry,' I muttered to myself as I descended to the door.

"'You'll have to wait until you bring home my clothes next week, Mrs. Blake.' I havn't any change this evening.'

"The expression of the poor woman's face, as she turned slowly away, without speaking, rather softened my feelings.

"'I'm sorry,' said I - 'but, it can't be helped now. I wish you had said, this morning, that you wanted money. I could have paid you then.'

"She paused, and turned partly towards me as I said this. Then she moved off, with something so sad in her manner, that I was touched, sensibly.

"'I ought to have paid her this morning when I had the change about me. And I wish I had done so. Why didn't she ask for her money if she wanted it so badly.'

"I felt, of coarse, rather ill at ease. A little while afterwards, I met the lady with whom I was boarding.

"'Do you know anything about this Mrs. Blake, who washes for me?' I enquired.

"'Not much; except that she is very poor, and has three children to feed and clothe. And what is worst of all, she is in bad health. I think she told me this morning, that one of her little ones was very sick.'

"I was smitten with a feeling of self-condemnation, and soon after left the room. It was too late to remedy the evil, for I had only a sixpence in my pocket; and, moreover, I did not know where to find Mrs. Blake. Having purposed to make a call upon some young ladies that evening, I now went up into my room to dress. Upon my bed lay the spotless linen brought home by Mrs. Blake in the morning. The sight of it rebuked me; and I had to conquer, with some force, an instinctive reluctance, before I could compel myself to put on a clean shirt, and snow-white vest, too recently from the hand of my unpaid washerwoman.

"One of the young ladies upon whom I called was more than a mere pleasant acquaintance. (And here Mr. Smith glanced, with a tender smile, towards me.) My heart had, in fact been warming towards her for some time; and I was particularly anxious to find favor in her eyes. On this evening she was lovelier and more attractive than ever.

"Judge then, of the effect produced upon me by the entrance of her mother - at the very moment when my heart was all a-glow with love, who said, as she came in -

"'Oh, dear! This is a strange world!'

"'What new feature have you discovered now, mother?' asked one of her daughters, smiling.

"'No new one, child; but an old one that looks more repulsive than ever,' was answered. 'Poor Mrs. Blake came to see me just now, in great trouble.'

"'What about, mother?' All the young ladies at once manifested unusual interest.

"Tell-tale blushes came instantly to my countenance, upon which the eyes of the mother turned themselves, as I felt, with a severe scrutiny.

"'The old story in cases like (sic) her's,' was answered. 'Can't get her money when earned, although, for daily bread, she is dependent on her daily labor. With no food in the house, or money to buy medicine for her sick child, she was compelled to seek me to-night, and to humble her spirit, which is an independent one, so low as to ask bread for her little ones, and the loan of a pittance with which to get what the doctor has ordered for her feeble sufferer at home.'

"'Oh, what a shame!' fell from the lips of her in whom my heart felt more than a passing interest; and she looked at me earnestly as she spoke.

"'She fully expected,' said the mother, 'to get a trifle that was due her from a young man who boards with Mrs. Corwin; and she went to see him this evening. But he put her off with some excuse. How strange that any one should be so thoughtless as to withhold from the poor their hard-earned pittance! It is but a small sum, at best, that the toiling seamstress or washer-woman can gain by her wearying labor. That, at least, should be promptly paid. To withhold it an hour is to do, in many cases, a great wrong.'

"For some minutes after this was said, there ensued a dead silence. I felt that the thoughts of all were turned upon me as the one who had withheld from poor Mrs. Blake the trifling sum due her for washing. What my feelings were, it is impossible for me to describe; and difficult for any one, never himself placed in so unpleasant a position, to imagine.

"My relief was great when the conversation flowed on again, and in another channel; for I then perceived that suspicion did not rest upon me. You may be sure that Mrs. Blake had her money before ten o'clock on the next day, and that I never again fell into the error of neglecting, for a single week, my poor washerwoman."

"Such a confession from you, Mr. Smith, of all men," said I, feeling a little uncomfortable, that he should have told this story of himself.

"We are none of us perfect," he answered, "He is best, who, conscious of natural defects and evils, strives against, and overcomes them."

CHAPTER XXVIII

MY BORROWING NEIGHBOR

"I THINK, my dear," said I to my husband one day, "that we shall have to move from here."

"Why so?" asked Mr. Smith, in surprise. "It is a very comfortable house. I am certain we will not get another as desirable at the same rent."

"I don't know that we will. But - "

Just as I said this, my cook opened the door of the room where we were sitting and said -

"Mrs. Jordon, ma'am, wants to borrow half a pound of butter. She says, they are entirely out, and their butter-man won't come before to-morrow."

"Very well, Bridget, let her have it."

The cook retired.

"Why do you wish to move, Jane?" asked my husband, as the girl closed the door.

"Cook's visit was quite apropos," I replied. "It is on account of the 'half pound of butter,' 'cup of sugar,' and 'pan of flour' nuisance."

T. S. Arthur

"I don't exactly comprehend you, Jane," said my husband.

"It is to get rid of a borrowing neighbor. The fact is, Mrs. Jordon is almost too much for me. I like to be accommodating; it gives me pleasure to oblige my neighbors; I am ready to give any reasonable obedience to the Scripture injunction - *from him that would borrow of thee, turn thou not away;* but Mrs. Jordon goes beyond all reason."

"Still, if she is punctual in returning what she gets, I don't know that you ought to let it annoy you a great deal."

"There lies the gist of the matter, my dear," I replied. "If there were no 'if,' such as you suggest, in the case, I would not think a great deal about it. But, the fact is, there is no telling the cups of sugar, pans of flour, pounds of butter, and little matters of salt, pepper, vinegar, mustard, ginger, spices, eggs, lard, meal, and the dear knows what all, that go out monthly, but never come back again. I verily believe we suffer through Mrs. Jordon's habit of borrowing not less than fifty or sixty dollars a year. Little things like these count up."

"So bad as that, is it?" said my husband.

"Indeed it is; and when she returns anything, it is almost always of an inferior quality, and frequently thrown away on that account."

While we were talking, the tea bell rang, and we retired to the dining-room.

"What's the matter with this tea?" asked Mr. Smith, pushing the cup I had handed him aside, after leaving sipped of its contents. "I never tasted such stuff. It's like herb tea."

"It must be something in the water," replied I. "The tea is the same we have been using all along."

I poured some into a cup and tasted it.

"Pah!" I said, with disgust, and rang the bell. The cook entered in a few moments.

"Bridget, what's the matter with your tea? It isn't fit to drink. Is it the same we have been using?"

"No, ma'am," replied Bridget. "It is some Mrs. Jordon sent home. I reminded Nancy, when she was here for butter, that they owed us some tea, borrowed day before yesterday, and she came right back with it, saying that Mrs. Jordon was sorry it had slipped her mind. I thought I would draw it by itself, and not mix it with the tea in our canister."

"You can throw this out and draw fresh tea, Bridget; we can't drink it," said I, handing her the tea-pot.

"You see how it works," I remarked as Bridget left the room, and my husband leaned back in his chair to wait for a fresh cup of tea. "One half of the time, when anything is returned, we can't use it. The butter Mrs. Jordon got a little while ago, if returned to-morrow, will not be fit to go on our table. We can only use it for cooking."

"It isn't right," sententiously remarked my husband. "The fact is," he resumed, after a slight pause, "I wouldn't lend such a woman anything. It is a downright imposition."

"It is a very easy thing to say that, Mr. Smith. But I am not prepared to do it. I don't believe Mrs. Jordon means to do wrong, or is really conscious that she is trespassing upon us. Some people don't reflect. Otherwise she is a pleasant neighbor, and I like her very much. It is want of proper thought, Mr. Smith, and nothing else."

"If a man kept treading on my gouty toe for want of thought," said my husband, "I should certainly tell him of it, whether he got offended I or not. If his friendship could only be retained on these terms, I would prefer dispensing with the favor."

T. S. Arthur

"The case isn't exactly parallel, Mr. Smith," was my reply. "The gouty toe and crushing heel are very palpable and straightforward matters, and a man would be an egregious blockhead to be offended when reminded of the pain he was inflicting. But it would be impossible to make Mrs. Jordon at all conscious of the extent of her short-comings, very many of which, in fact, are indirect, so far as she is concerned, and arise from her general sanction of the borrowing system. I do not suppose, for a moment, that she knows about everything that is borrowed."

"If she dosn't, pray who does?" inquired my husband.

"Her servants. I have to be as watchful as you can imagine, to see that Bridget, excellent a girl as she is, doesn't suffer things to get out, and then, at the last moment, when it is too late to send to the store, run in to a neighbor's and borrow to hide her neglect. If I gave her a *carte blanche* for borrowing, I might be as annoying to my neighbors as Mrs. Jordon."

"That's a rather serious matter," said my husband. "In fact, there is no knowing how much people may suffer in their neighbors' good opinion, through the misconduct of their servants in this very thing."

"Truly said. And now let me relate a fact about Mrs. Jordon, that illustrates your remark." (The fresh tea had come in, and we were going on with our evening meal.) "A few weeks ago we had some friends here, spending the evening. When about serving refreshments, I discovered that my two dozen tumblers had been reduced to seven or eight. On inquiry, I learned that Mrs. Jordon had ten - the rest had been broken. I sent to her, with my compliments, and asked her to return them, as I had some company, and wished to use them in serving refreshments. Bridget was gone some time, and when she returned, said that Mrs. Jordon at first denied having any of my tumblers. Her cook was called, who acknowledged to five, and, after sundry efforts on the part of Bridget to refresh her memory, finally gave in to the whole ten. Early on the next morning Mrs. Jordon came in to see me, and seemed a good deal mortified about the tumblers.

"'It was the first I had heard about it,' she said. 'Nancy, it now appears, borrowed of you to hide her own breakage, and I should have been none the wiser, if you had not sent in. I have not a single tumbler left. It is too bad! I don't care so much for the loss of the tumblers, as I do for the mortifying position it placed me in toward a neighbor.'"

"Upon my word!" exclaimed my husband. "That is a beautiful illustration, sure enough, of my remarks about what people may suffer in the good opinion of others, through the conduct of their servants in this very thing. No doubt Mrs. Jordon, as you suggest, is guiltless of a good deal of blame now laid at her door. It was a fair opportunity for you to give her some hints on the subject. You might have opened her eyes a little, or at least diminished the annoyance you had been, and still are enduring."

"Yes, the opportunity was a good one, and I ought to have improved it. But I did not and the whole system, sanctioned or not sanctioned by Mrs. Jordon, is in force against me."

"And will continue, unless some means be adopted by which to abate the nuisance."

"Seriously, Mr. Smith," said I, "I am clear for removing from the neighborhood."

But Mr. Smith said,

"Nonsense, Jane!" A form of expression he uses, when he wishes to say that my proposition or suggestion is perfectly ridiculous, and not to be thought of for a moment.

"What is to be done?" I asked. "Bear the evil?"

"Correct it, if you can."

T. S. Arthur

"And if not, bear it the best I can?"

"Yes, that is my advice."

This was about the extent of aid I ever received from my husband in any of my domestic difficulties. He is a first-rate abstractionist, and can see to a hair how others ought to act in every imaginable, and I was going to say unimaginable case; but is just as backward about telling people what he thinks of them, and making everybody with whom he has anything to do toe the mark, as I am.

As the idea of moving to get rid of my borrowing neighbor was considered perfect nonsense by Mr. Smith, I began to think seriously how I should check the evil, now grown almost insufferable. On the next morning the coffee-mill was borrowed to begin with.

"Hasn't Mrs. Jordon got a coffee-mill of her own?" I asked of Bridget.

"Yes, ma'am," she replied, "but it is such a poor one that Nancy won't use it. She says it takes her forever and a day to grind enough coffee for breakfast."

"Does she get ours every morning?"

"Yes, ma'am."

Nancy opened the kitchen door at this moment - our back gates were side by side - and said -

"Mrs. Jordon says, will you oblige her so much as to let her have an egg to clear the coffee? I forgot to tell her yesterday that ours were all gone."

"Certainly," I said. "Bridget, give Nancy an egg."

"Mrs. Jordon is very sorry to trouble you, Mrs. Smith," said

Nancy, re-appearing in a little while, and finding me still in the kitchen, "but she says if you will lend her a bowl of sugar it will be a great accommodation. I forgot to tell her yesterday that the sugar was all gone."

"You appear to be rather forgetful of such matters, Nancy," I could not help saying.

"I know I am a little forgetful," the girl said, good humoredly, but I have so much to do, that I hardly have time to think."

"Where is the large earthen dish that you use sometimes in making bread?" I asked, after Mrs. Jordon's cook had withdrawn, missing it from its usual place on the shelf.

"Nancy borrowed it last week."

"Why don't she bring it home?"

"I've told her about it three or four times."

Nancy opened the door again.

"Please, ma'am to let Mrs. Jordon have another half pound of butter. We haven't enough to do for breakfast, and the butter man don't come until the middle of the day."

Of course, I couldn't refuse, though I believe I granted the request with no very smiling grace. I heard no more of Nancy until toward dinner-time. I had given my cook orders not to lend her anything more without first coming to me.

"Mrs. Jordon has sent in to know if you won't lend her two or three scuttles full of coal," said Bridget. "Mr. Jordon was to have sent home the fires are going down."

"Certainly," I replied, "let her have it, but I want you to see that it is returned."

"As to that, ma'am, I'll do my best; but I can't get Nancy to return one half what she borrows. She forgets from one day to another."

"She mustn't forget," I returned, warmly. "You must go to Mrs. Jordon yourself. It isn't right."

"I shall have to go, I guess, before I'm able to get back a dozen kitchen things of ours they have. I never saw such borrowing people. And then, never to think of returning what they get. They have got one of our pokers, the big sauce-pan and the cake-board. Our muffin rings they've had these three months. Every Monday they get two of our tubs and the wash-boiler. Yesterday they sent in and got our large meat-dish belonging to the dinner-set, and haven't sent it home yet. Indeed, I can't tell you all they've got."

"Let Nancy have the coal," said I. "But we must stop this in some way, if it be possible."

For three or four days the same thing was kept up, until I lost all patience, and resolved, offence or no offence, to end a system that was both annoying and unjust.

Mrs. Jordon called in to see me one day, and sat conversing in a very pleasant strain for an hour. She was an agreeable companion, and I was pleased with the visit. In fact, I liked Mrs. Jordon.

About an hour after she was gone, Nancy came into the kitchen, where I happened to be.

"What's wanted now?" said I. My voice expressed quite as much as my words. I saw the color flush in Nancy's face.

"Mrs. Jordon says, will you please to lend her a pan of flour? She will return it to-morrow."

"Tell Mrs. Jordon," I replied, "that we are going to make up bread this afternoon, and haven't more than enough flour left, or I would let her have what she wants. And, by the way, Nancy, tell Mrs. Jordon that I will be obliged to her if she will send in my large earthen dish. We want to use it."

Nancy didn't seem pleased. And I thought she muttered something to herself as she went away.

Not five minutes elapsed before word came to my room that Mrs. Jordon was in the parlor and wished to speak to me.

"Now for trouble," thought I. Sure enough, when I entered the parlor, the knit brow, flushed face, and angry eyes of my neighbor told me that there was to be a scene.

"Mrs. Smith," she began, without ceremony or apology for her abruptness of manner, "I should like to know what you mean by the manner in which you refused to let me have a little flour just now?"

"How did I refuse?" I was cool enough to inquire.

"You refused in a manner which plainly enough snowed that you thought me a troublesome borrower. 'What's wanted now?' I think rather strange language to use to a domestic of mine."

Really, thought I, this caps the climax.

"To speak the plain truth, Mrs. Jordon," said I, "and not wishing to give any offence, you do use the privilege of a neighbor in this respect rather freely - more freely, I must own, than I feel justified in doing."

"Mrs. Smith, this is too much!" exclaimed Mrs. Jordon. "Why you borrow of me twice where I borrow of you once. I am particularly careful in matters of this kind."

I looked at the woman with amazement.

T. S. Arthur

"Borrow of you?" I asked.

"Certainly!" she replied, with perfect coolness. "Scarcely a day passes that you do not send in for something or other. But dear knows! I have always felt pleasure in obliging you."

I was mute for a time.

"Really, Mrs. Jordon," said I, at length, as composedly as I could speak, "you seem to be laboring under some strange mistake. The charge of frequent borrowing, I imagine, lies all on the other side. I can name a dozen of my things in your house now, and can mention as many articles borrowed within the last three days."

"Pray do so," was her cool reply.

"You have my large wash-boiler," I replied, "and two of my washing tubs. You borrow them every Monday, and I have almost always to send for them."

"I have your wash-boiler and tubs? You are in error, Mrs. Smith. I have a large boiler of my own, and plenty of tubs."

"I don't know what you have, Mrs. Jordon; but I do know that you get mine every week. Excuse me for mentioning these things - I do so at your desire. Then, there is my coffee-mill, borrowed every morning."

"Coffee-mill! Why should I borrow your coffee-mill? We have one of our own."

"Yesterday you borrowed butter, and eggs, and sugar," I continued.

"I?" my neighbor seemed perfectly amazed.

"Yes; and the day before a loaf of bread - an egg to clear your coffee - salt, pepper, and a nutmeg."

"Never!"

"And to-day Nancy got some lard, a cup of coffee, and some Indian meal for a pudding."

"She did?" asked Mrs. Jordon in a quick voice, a light seeming to have flashed upon her mind.

"Yes," I replied, "for I was in the kitchen when she got the lard and meal, and Bridget mentioned the coffee as soon as I came down this morning."

"Strange!" Mrs. Jordon looked thoughtful. "It isn't a week since we got coffee, and I am sure our Indian meal cannot be out."

"Almost every week Nancy borrows a pound or a half pound of butter on the day before your butter man comes; and more than that, doesn't return it, or indeed anything she gets more than a third of the time."

"Precisely the complaint I have to make against you," said Mrs. Jordon, looking me steadily in the face.

"Then," said I "there is something wrong somewhere, for to my knowledge nothing has been borrowed from you or any body else for months. I forbid anything of the kind."

"Be that as it may, Mrs. Smith; Nancy frequently comes to me and says you have sent in for this, that, and the other thing - coffee, tea, sugar, butter; and, in fact, almost everything used in a family."

"Then Nancy gets them for her own use," said I.

"But I have often seen Bridget in myself for things."

"My Bridget!" I said, in surprise.

T. S. Arthur

I instantly rang the bell.

"Tell Bridget I want her," said I to the waiter who came to the door. The cook soon appeared.

"Bridget, are you in the habit of borrowing from Mrs. Jordon without my knowledge?"

"No, ma'am!" replied the girl firmly, and without any mark of disturbance in her face.

"Din't you get a bar of soap from our house yesterday?" asked Mrs. Jordon.

"Yes, ma'am," returned Bridget, "but it was soap you owed us."

"Owed you!"

"Yes, Ma am. Nancy got a bar of soap from me last washing-day, and I went in for it yesterday."

"But Nancy told me you wanted to borrow it," said Mrs. Jordon.

"Nancy knew better," said Bridget, with a face slightly flushed; but any one could see that it was a flush of indignation.

"Will you step into my house and tell Nancy I want to see her?"

"Certainly, ma'am." And Bridget retired.

"These servants have been playing a high game, I fear," remarked Mrs. Jordon, after Bridget had left the room. "Pardon me, if in my surprise I have spoken in a manner that has seemed offensive."

"Most certainly there is a game playing that I know nothing

about, if anything has been borrowed of you in my name for these three months," said I.

"I have heard of your borrowing something or other almost every day during the time you mention," replied Mrs. Jordon. "As for me, I have sent into you a few times; but not oftener, I am sure, than once in a week."

Bridget returned, after having been gone several minutes, and said Nancy would be in directly. We waited for some time, and then sent for her again. Word was brought back that she was nowhere to be found in the house.

"Come in with me, Mrs. Smith," said my neighbor, rising. I did so, according to her request. Sure enough, Nancy was gone. We went up into her room, and found that she had bundled up her clothes and taken them off, but left behind her unmistakable evidence of what she had been doing. In an old chest which Mrs. Jordon had let her use for her clothes were many packages of tea, burnt coffee, sugar, soap, eggs; a tin kettle containing a pound of butter, and various other articles of table use.

Poor Mrs. Jordon seemed bewildered.

"Let me look at that pound lump of butter," said I.

Mrs. Jordon took up the kettle containing it. "It isn't my butter," she remarked.

"But it's mine, and the very pound she got of me yesterday for you."

"Gracious me!" ejaculated my neighbor. "Was anything like this ever heard?"

"She evidently borrowed on your credit and mine - both ways," I remarked with a smile, for all my unkind feelings toward Mrs. Jordon were gone, "and for her own benefit."

T. S. Arthur

"But isn't it dreadful to think of, Mrs. Smith? See what harm the creature has done! Over and over again have I complained of your borrowing so much and returning so little; and you have doubtless made the same complaint of me."

"I certainly have. I felt that I was not justly dealt by."

"It makes me sick to think of it." And Mrs. Jordon sank into a chair.

"Still I don't understand about the wash-boiler and tubs that you mentioned," she said, after a pause.

"You remember my ten tumblers," I remarked.

"Perfectly. But can she have broken up my tubs and boiler, or carried them off?"

On searching in the cellar we found the tubs in ruins, and the wash-boiler with a large hole in the bottom.

I shall never forget the chagrin, anger, and mortification of poor Mrs. Jordon when, at her request, Bridget pointed out at least twenty of my domestic utensils that Nancy had borrowed to replace such as she had broken or carried away. (It was a rule with Mrs. Jordon to make her servants pay for every thing they broke.)

"To think of it!" she repeated over and over again. "Just to think of it! Who could have dreamed of such doings?"

Mrs. Jordon was, in fact, as guiltless of the sin of troublesome borrowing from a neighbor as myself. And yet I had seriously urged the propriety of moving out of the neighborhood to get away from her.

We both looked more closely to the doings of our servants after this pretty severe lesson; and I must freely confess, that in my own case, the result was worth all the trouble. As trusty a girl as my cook was, I found that she would occasionally run in to a neighbor's to borrow something or other, in order to hide her own neglect; and I only succeeded in stopping the the evil by threatening to send her away if I ever detected her in doing it again.

T. S. Arthur

CHAPTER XXIX

EXPERIENCE IN TAKING BOARDERS

I HAVE no experiences of my own to relate on this subject. But I could fill a book with the experiences of my friends. How many poor widows, in the hope of sustaining their families and educating their children, have tried the illusive, and, at best, doubtful experiment of taking boarders, to find themselves in a year or two, or three, hopelessly involved in debt, a life time of labor would fail to cancel. Many, from pride, resort to this means of getting a living, because - why I never could comprehend - taking boarders is thought to be more genteel than needlework or keeping a small store for the sale of fancy articles.

The experience of one of my friends, a Mrs. Turner, who, in the earlier days of her sad widowhood, found it needful to make personal effort for the sustenance of her family, I will here relate. Many who find themselves in trying positions like hers, may, in reviewing her mistakes, be saved from similar ones themselves.

"I don't know what we shall do!" exclaimed Mrs. Turner, about six months after the death of her husband, while pondering sadly over the prospect before her. She had one daughter about twenty, and two sons who were both under ten years of age. Up to this time she had never known the dread of want. Her husband had been able to provide well for his family; and they moved in a very respectable, and somewhat showy circle. But on his death, his affairs were found to be much involved, and when settled, there was left for the widow and children only about the sum of four thousand dollars, besides the household furniture, which was very handsome. This sad falling off in her prospects, had been communicated to Mrs. Turner a short time before, by the administrator on the estate; and its effect was to alarm and sadden her extremely. She knew nothing of business, and yet, was painfully conscious, that four thousand dollars would be but a trifle to what she would need for her family, and that effort in some direction was now absolutely necessary. But, besides her ignorance of any calling by which money could be made, she had a superabundance of false pride, and shrunk from what she was pleased to consider the odium attached to a woman who had to engage in business. Under these circumstances, she had a poor enough prospect before her. The exclamation as above recorded, was made in the presence of Mary Turner, her daughter, a well educated girl, who had less of that false pride which obscured her mother's perceptions of right. After a few moments' silence the latter said -

"And yet we must do something, mother."

"I know that, Mary, too well. But I know of nothing that we can do."

"Suppose we open a little dry goods' store?" suggested Mary. "Others seem to do well at it, and we might. You know we have a great many friends."

"Don't think of it, Mary! We could not expose ourselves in that way."

"I know that it would not be pleasant, mother; but, then, we must do something."

"It must be something besides that, Mary. I can't listen to it. It's only a vulgar class of women who keep stores."

T. S. Arthur

"I am willing to take in sewing, mother; but, then, all I could earn would go but a little way towards keeping the family. I don't suppose I could even pay the rent, and that you know, is four hundred dollars."

"Too true," Mrs. Turner said, despondingly.

"Suppose I open a school?" suggested Mary.

"O no! no! My head would never stand the noise and confusion. And, any way, I never did like a school."

"Then I don't know what we shall do, unless we take some boarders."

"A little more genteel. But even that is low enough."

"Then, suppose, mother we look for a lower rent, and try to live more economically. I will take in sewing, and we can try for awhile, and see how we get along."

"O no, indeed, child. That would never do. We must keep up appearances, or we shall lose our place in society. You know that it is absolutely necessary for you and your brothers, that we should maintain our position."

"As for me, mother," said Mary, in a serious tone, "I would not have you to take a thought in that direction. And it seems to me that our true position is the one where we can live most comfortably according to our means."

"You don't know anything about it, child," Mrs. Turner replied, in a positive tone.

Mary was silenced for the time. But a banishment of the subject did not, in any way, lesson the difficulties. Thoughts of these soon again became apparent in words; and the most natural form of these was the sentence -

"I don't know what we *shall* do!" uttered by the mother in a tone of deep despondency.

"Suppose we take a few boarders?" Mary urged, about three weeks after the conversation just alluded to.

"No, Mary; we would be too much exposed: and then it would come very hard on you, for you know that I cannot stand much fatigue," Mrs. Turner replied, slowly and sadly.

"O, as to that," said Mary, with animation: "I'll take all the burden off of you."

"Indeed, child, I cannot think of it," Mrs. Turner replied, positively; and again the subject was dismissed.

But it was soon again recurred to, and after the suggestion and disapproval of many plans, Mary again said -

"Indeed, mother, I don't see what we will do, unless we take a few boarders."

"It's the only thing at all respectable, that I can think of," Mrs. Turner said despondingly; "and I'm afraid it's the best we can do."

"I think we had better try it, mother, don't you?"

"Well, perhaps we had, Mary. There are four rooms that we can spare; and these ought to bring us in something handsome."

"What ought we to charge?"

"About three dollars and a half for young men, and ten dollars for a man and his wife."

"If we could get four married couples for the four rooms, that would be forty dollars a week, which would be pretty good," said Mary, warming at the thought.

"Yes, if we could, Mary, we might manage pretty well. But most married people have children, and they are such an annoyance that I wouldn't have them in the house. We will have to depend mainly on the young men."

It was, probably, three weeks after this, that an advertisement, running thus, appeared in one of the newspapers:

"BOARDING - Five or six genteel young men, or a few gentlemen and their wives, can be accommodated with boarding at No. - Cedar street. Terms moderate."

In the course of the following day, a man called and asked the terms for himself and wife.

"Ten dollars," said Mrs. Turner.

"That's too high - is it not?" remarked the man.

"We cannot take you for less."

"Have you a pleasant room vacant?"

"You can have your choice of the finest in the house?"

"Can I look at them, madam?"

"Certainly, sir." And the stranger was taken through Mrs. Turner's beautifully furnished chambers.

"Well, this is certainly a temptation," said the man, pausing and looking around the front chamber on the second floor. "And you have named your lowest terms?"

"Yes, sir; the lowest."

"Well, it's higher than I've been paying, but this looks too comfortable. I suppose we will have to strike a bargain."

"Shall be pleased to accommodate you, sir."

"We will come, then, to-morrow morning."

"Very well, sir." And the stranger departed.

"So much for a beginning," said Mrs. Turner, evidently gratified. "He seems to be much of a gentleman. If his wife is like him, they will make things very agreeable I am sure."

"I hope she is," said Mary.

On the next morning, the new boarders made their appearance, and the lady proved as affable and as interesting as the husband.

"I always pay quarterly. This is the custom in all the boarding houses I have been in. But if your rules are otherwise, why just say so. It makes no difference to me," remarked the new boarder, in the blandest manner imaginable.

"Just suit yourself about that, Mr. Cameron. It is altogether immaterial," Mrs. Turner replied, smiling. "I am in no particular want of money."

Mr. Cameron bowed lower, and smiled more blandly, if possible, than before.

"You have just opened a boarding house, I suppose, madam?" he said.

"Yes sir, I am a new beginner at the business."

"Ah - well, I must try and make you known all I can. You will find Mrs. Cameron, here, a sociable kind of a woman. And if I can serve you at any time, be sure to command me."

T. S. Arthur

"You are too kind!" Mrs. Turner responded, much pleased to have found, in her first boarders, such excellent, good-hearted people.

In a few days, a couple of young men made application, and were received, and now commenced the serious duties of the new undertaking. Mary had to assume the whole care of the house. She had to attend the markets, and oversee the kitchen, and also to make with her own hands all the pastry. Still, she had, a willing heart, and this lightened much of the heavy burden now imposed upon her.

"How do you like your new boarding house?" asked a friend of one of the young men who had applied, and been received. This was about two weeks after his entrance into Mrs. Turner's house.

"Elegant," responded the young man, giving his countenance a peculiar and knowing expression.

"Indeed? But are you in earnest?"

"I am that. Why, we live on the very fat of the land."

"Pshaw! you must be joking. Whoever heard of the fat of the land being found in a boarding house. They can't afford it."

"I don't care, myself, whether they can afford it or not. But we do live elegantly. I wouldn't ask to sit down to a better table."

"What kind of a room have you? and what kind of a bed?"

"Good enough for a lord."

"Nonsense!"

"No, but I am in earnest, as I will prove to you. I sleep on as fine a bed as ever I saw, laid on a richly carved mahogany bedstead, with beautiful curtains. The floor is covered with a

Brussels carpet, nearly new and of a rich pattern. There is in the room a mahogany wardrobe, an elegant piece of furniture - a marble top dressing bureau, and a mahogany wash-stand with a marble slab. Now if you don't call that a touch above a common boarding house, you've been more fortunate than I have been until lately."

"Are there any vacancies there, Tom?"

"There is another bed in my room."

Well, just tell them, to-night, that I'll be there to-morrow morning."

"Very well."

"And I know of a couple more that'll add to the mess, if there is room."

"It's a large house, and I believe they have room yet to spare."

A week more passed away, and the house had its complement, six young men, and the polite gentleman and his wife. This promised an income of thirty-one dollars per week.

As an off-set to this, a careful examination into the weekly expenditure would have shown a statement something like the following: Marketing $12; groceries, flour, &c., $10; rent, $8; servants' hire-cook, chambermaid, and black boy, $4; fuel, and incidental expenses, $6 - in all, $40 per week. Besides this, their own clothes, and the schooling of the two boys did not cost less than at the rate of $300 per annum. But neither Mrs. Turner nor Mary ever thought that any such calculation was necessary. They charged what other boarding house keepers charged, and thought, of course, that they must make a good living. But in no boarding house, even where much higher prices were obtained, was so much piled upon the table.

Every thing, in its season, was to be found there, without

regard to prices. Of course, the boarders were delighted, and complimented Mrs. Turner upon the excellent fare which they received.

Mr. and Mrs. Cameron continued as affable and interesting as when they first came into the house. But the first quarter passed away, and nothing was said about their bill, and Mrs. Turner never thought of giving them a polite hint. Two of her young men were also remiss in this respect, but they were such gentlemanly, polite, attentive individuals, that, of course, nothing could be said.

"I believe I've never had your bill, Mrs. Turner, have I?" Mr. Cameron said to her one evening, when about six months had passed.

"No; I have never thought of handing it in. But it's no difference, I'm not in want of money."

"Yes, but it ought to be paid. I'll bring you up a check from the counting-room in a few days."

"Suit your own convenience, Mr. Cameron," answered Mrs. Turner, in an indifferent tone.

"O, it's perfectly convenient at all times. But knowing that you were not in want of it, has made me negligent."

This was all that was said on the subject for another quarter, during which time the two young men alluded to as being in arrears, went off, cheating the widow out of fifty dollars each.

But nothing was said about it to the other boarders, and none of them knew of the wrong that had been sustained. Their places did not fill up, and the promised weekly income was reduced to twenty-four dollars.

At the end of the third quarter, Mr. Cameron again recollected that he had neglected to bring up a check from the counting-room, and blamed himself for his thoughtlessness.

"I am so full of business," said he, "that I sometimes neglect these little things."

"But it's a downright shame, Mr. Cameron, when it's so easy for you to draw off a check and put it into your pocket," remarked his wife.

"O, it's not a particle of difference," Mrs. Turner volunteered to say, smiling - though, to tell the truth, she would much rather have had the money.

"Well, I'll try and bear it in mind this very night," and Mr. Cameron hurried away, as business pressed.

The morning after Mr. Cameron's fourth quarter expired, he walked out, as usual, with his wife before breakfast. But when all assembled at the table, they had not (something very uncommon for them) returned.

"I wonder what keeps Mr. and Mrs. Cameron?" remarked Mrs. Turner.

"Why, I saw them leave in the steamboat for the South, this morning," said one of the boarders.

"You must be mistaken," Mrs. Turner replied.

"O no, ma'am, not at all. I saw them, and conversed with them before the boat started. They told me that they were going on as far as Washington."

"Very strange!" ejaculated Mrs. Turner. "They said nothing to me about it."

"I hope they don't owe you any thing," remarked one of the boarders.

"Indeed, they do."

"Not much, ma'am; I hope."

"Over five hundred dollars."

"O, that is too bad! How could you trust a man like Mr. Cameron to such an amount?"

"Why, surely," said Mrs. Turner, "he is a respectable and a responsible merchant; and I was in no want of the money."

"Indeed, Mrs. Turner, he is no such thing."

"Then what is he?"

"He is one of your gentlemen about town, and lives, I suppose, by gambling. At least such is the reputation he bears. I thought you perfectly understood this."

"How cruelly I have been deceived!" said Mrs. Turner, unable to command her feelings; and rising, she left the table in charge of Mary.

On examining Mr. and Mrs. Cameron's room, their trunk was found, but it was empty. The owners of it, of course, came not back to claim their property.

The result of this year's experience in keeping boarders, was an income of just $886 in money, and a loss of $600, set off against an expense of $2380. Thus was Mrs. Turner worse off by $1494 at the end of the year, than she was when she commenced keeping boarders. But she made no estimates, and had not the most remote idea of how the matter stood. Whenever she wanted money, she drew upon the amount placed to her credit in bank by the administrator on her husband's estate, vainly imagining that it would all come back through the boarders. All that she supposed to be lost of the first year's business were the $600, out of which she had been cheated. Resolving to be more circumspect in future, another year was entered upon. But she could not help seeing that Mary was suffering from hard labor and close confinement, and it pained her exceedingly. One day she said to her, a few weeks after they had entered upon the second year -

"I am afraid, Mary, this is too hard for you. You begin to look pale and thin. You must spare yourself more."

"I believe I do need a little rest, mother," said Mary; "but if I don't look after things, nobody will, and then we should soon have our boarders dissatisfied."

"That is too true, Mary."

"But I wouldn't mind it so much, mother, if I thought we were getting ahead. But I am afraid we are not."

"What makes you think so, child?"

"You know we have lost six hundred dollars already, and that is a great deal of money."

"True, Mary; but we must be more careful in future. We will soon make that up, I am sure."

"I hope so," Mary responded, with a sigh. She did not herself feel so sanguine of making it up. Still, she had not entered into any calculation of income and expense, leaving that to her mother, and supposing that all was right as a matter of course.

As they continued to set an excellent table, they kept up pretty regularly their complement of boarders. The end of the second year would have shown this result, if a calculation had been made: cash income, $1306 - loss by boarders, $150 - whole expenses, $2000. Consequently, they were worse off at the end of the year by $694; or in the two years, $2188, by keeping boarders.

And now poor Mrs. Turner was startled on receiving her bank book from the bank, settled up, to find that her four thousand dollars had dwindled down to $1812. She could not at first believe her senses. But there were all her checks regularly entered; and, to dash even the hope that there was a mistake, there were the cancelled checks, also, bearing her own signature.

"Mary, what *shall* we do?" was her despairing question, as the full truth became distinct to her mind.

"You say we have sunk more than two thousand dollars in two years?"

"Yes, my child."

"And have had all our hard labor for nothing?" Mary continued, and her voice trembled as she thought of how much she had gone through in that time.

"Yes."

"Something must be wrong, mother. Let us do what we should have done at first, make a careful estimate of our expenses."

"Well."

"It costs us just ten dollars each week for marketing - and I know that our groceries are at least that, including flour; that you see makes twenty dollars, and we only get twenty-eight dollars for our eight boarders. Our rent will bring our expenses up to that. And then there are servants' wages, fuel, our own clothes, and the boys' schooling, besides what we lose every year, and the hundred little expenses which cannot be enumerated."

"Bless me, Mary! No wonder we have gone behindhand."

"Indeed, mother, it is not."

"We have acted very blindly, Mary."

"Yes, we have; but we must do so no longer. Let us give up our boarders, and move into a smaller house."

"But what shall we do Mary? Our money will soon dwindle away."

"We must do something for a living, mother, that is true. But if we cannot now see what we shall do, that is no reason why we should go on as we are. Our rent, you know, takes away from us eight dollars a week. We can get a house large enough for our own purposes at three dollars a week, or one hundred and fifty dollars a year, I am sure, thus saving five dollars a week there, and that money would buy all the plain food our whole family would eat."

"But it will never do, Mary, for us to go to moving into a little bit of a pigeon-box of a house."

"Mother, if we don't get into a cheaper house and husband our resources, we shall soon have no house to live in!" said Mary, with unwonted energy.

"Well, child, perhaps you are right; but I can't bear the thought of it," Mrs. Turner replied. "And any how, I can't see what we are going to do then."

"We ought to do what we see to be right, mother, had we not?" Mary asked, looking affectionately into her mother's face.

"I suppose so, Mary."

"Won't it be right for us to reduce our expenses, and make the most of what we have left?"

"It certainly will, Mary."

T. S. Arthur

"Then let us do what seems to be right, and we shall see further, I am sure, as soon as we have acted."

Thus urged, Mrs. Turner consented to relinquish her boarders, and to move into a small house, at a rent very considerably reduced.

Many articles of furniture they were obliged to dispose of, and this added to their little fund some five hundred dollars. About two months after they were fairly settled, Mary said to her mother -

"I've been thinking a good deal lately, mother, about getting into something that would bring us in a living."

"Well, child, what conclusion have you come to?"

"You don't like the idea of setting up a little store?"

"No, Mary, it is too exposing."

"Nor of keeping a school?"

"No."

"Well, what do you think of my learning the dress-making business?"

"Nonsense, Mary!"

"But, mother, I could learn in six months, and then we could set up the business, and I am sure we could do well. Almost every one who sets up dress-making, gets along."

"There was always something low to me in the idea of a milliner or mantua maker, and I cannot bear the thought of your being one," Mrs. Turner replied, in a decided tone.

"You know what Pope says, mother -

'Honor and shame from no *condition* rise;
Act well your part, there all the honor lies.'"

"Yes, but that is poetry, child."

"And song is but the eloquence of truth, some one has beautifully said," responded Mary, smiling.

The mother was silent, and Mary, whose mind had never imbibed, fully, her mother's false notions, continued -

"I am sure there can be no wrong in my making dresses. Some one must make them, and it is the end we have in view, it seems to me, that determines the character of an action. If I, for the sake of procuring an honest living for my mother, my little brothers, and myself, am willing to devote my time to dress-making, instead of sitting in idleness, and suffering James and Willie to be put out among strangers, then the calling is to me honorable. My aim is honorable, and the means are honest. Is it not so, mother?"

"Yes, I suppose it is so. But then there was always something so degrading to me in the idea of being nothing but a dress-maker!"

Just at that moment a young man, named Martin, who had lived with them during the last year of their experiment in keeping boarders, called in to see them. He kept a store in the city, and was reputed to be well off. He had uniformly manifested an interest in Mrs. Turner and her family, and was much liked by them. After he was seated. Mrs. Turner said to him -

"I am trying, Mr. Martin, to beat a strange notion out of Mary's head. She has been endeavouring to persuade me to let her learn the dress-making business."

The young man seemed a little surprised at this communication, and Mary evinced a momentary confusion when it was made. He said, however, very promptly and pleasantly, turning to Mary -

"I suppose you have a good reason for it, Miss Mary."

"I think I have, Mr. Martin," she replied, smiling. "We cannot live, and educate James and William, unless we have a regular income; and I cannot shut my eyes to the fact that what we have cannot last long - nor to another, that I am the only one in the family from whom any regular income can be expected."

"And you are willing to devote yourself to incessant toil, night and day, for this purpose?"

"Certainly I am," Mary replied, with a quiet, cheerful smile.

"But it never will do, Mr. Martin, will it?" Mrs. Turner remarked.

"Why not, Mrs. Turner?"

"Because, it is not altogether respectable."

"I do not see any thing disrespectable in the business; but, with Mary's motive for entering into it, something highly respectable and honorable," Mr. Martin replied, with unusual earnestness.

Mrs. Turner was silenced.

"And you really think of learning the business, and then setting it up?" said Mr. Martin, turning to Mary, with a manifest interest, which she felt, rather than perceived.

"Certainly I do, if mother does not positively object."

"Then I wish you all success in your praiseworthy undertaking. And may the end you have in view support you amid the wearisome toil."

There was a peculiar feeling in Mr. Martin's tone that touched the heart of Mary, she knew not why. But certain it was, that she felt doubly nerved for the task she had proposed to herself.

As Mr. Martin wended his way homeward that evening, he thought of Mary Turner with an interest new to him. He had never been a great deal in her company while he boarded with her mother, because Mary was always too busy about household affairs, to be much in the parlor. But what little he had seen of her, made him like her as a friend. He also liked Mrs. Turner, and had from these reasons, frequently called in to see them since their removal. After going into his room, on his return home that evening, he sat down and remained for some time in a musing attitude. At length he got up, and took a few turns across the floor, and again seated himself, saying as he did so -

"If that's the stuff she's made of, she's worth looking after."

From this period, Mr. Martin called to see Mrs. Turner more frequently, and as Mary, who had promptly entered upon the duties of a dress-maker's apprentice, came home every evening, he had as many opportunities of being with her and conversing with her as he desired. Amiable accomplished, and intelligent, she failed not to make, unconsciously to herself, a decided impression upon the young man's heart. Nor could she conceal from herself that she was (sic) happier in his company than she was at any other time.

Week after week, and month after month, passed quickly away, and Mary was rapidly acquiring a skill in the art she was learning, rarely obtained by any. After the end of four months, she could turn off a dress equal to any one in the work-room. But this constant application was making sad inroads upon her health. For two years she had been engaged in active and laborious duties, even beyond her strength. The change from this condition to the perfectly sedentary, was more than her constitution could bear up under, especially as she was compelled to bend over her needle regularly, from ten to twelve hours each day. As the time for the expiration of her term of service approached, she felt her strength to be fast failing her. Her cheek had become paler and thinner, her step more languid, and her appetite was almost entirely gone.

These indications of failing health were not unobserved by Mr. Martin. But, not having made up his mind, definitely, that she was precisely the woman he wanted for a wife, he could not interfere to prevent her continuance at the business which was too evidently destroying her health. But every time he saw her his interest in her became tenderer. "If no one steps forward and saves her," he would sometimes say to himself, as he gazed with saddened feelings upon her colorless cheek, "she will fall a victim in the very bloom of womanhood."

And Mary herself saw the sad prospect before her. She told no one of the pain in her side, nor of the sickening sensation of weakness and weariness that daily oppressed her. But she toiled on and on, hoping to feel better soon. At last her probation ended. But the determined and ambitious spirit that had kept her up, now gave way.

Martin knew the day when her apprenticeship expired, and without asking why, followed the impulse that prompted him, and called upon her in the evening.

"Is any thing the matter, Mrs. Turner?" he asked, with a feeling of alarm, on entering the house and catching a glance at the expression of that lady's countenance.

"Oh, yes, Mr. Martin, Mary is extremely ill," she replied, in evident painful anxiety.

"What ails her?" he asked, showing equal concern.

"I do not know, Mr. Martin. She came home this evening, and as soon as she reached her chamber fainted away. I sent for the doctor immediately, and he says that she must be kept very quiet, and that he will be here very early in the morning again.

I am afraid she has overworked herself. Indeed, I am sure she has. For many weeks back, I have noticed her altered appearance and loss of appetite. It was in vain that I urged her to spare herself for a few weeks and make up the time afterwards. She steadily urged the necessity of getting into business as soon as possible, and would not give up. She has sacrificed herself, Mr. Martin, I very much fear, to her devotion to the family." And Mrs. Turner burst into tears.

We need not say how sad and depressed Martin was, on turning away from the house, without the chance of seeing Mary, under the idea, too, of her dangerous illness. He called about ten o'clock the next morning, and learned that she was no better; that the doctor had been there, and pronounced her in a low nervous fever. Strict injunctions had been left that no one should be admitted to her room but the necessary attendants.

Regularly every morning and evening Martin called to ask after Mary, for the space of fifteen days, and always received the sad information that she was no better. His feelings had now become intensely excited. He blamed himself for having favored the idea of Mary's going to learn a trade.

"How easily I might have prevented it!" he said to himself. "How blind I was to her true worth! How much suffering and toil I might have saved her!"

On the evening of the sixteenth day, he received the glad intelligence that Mary was better. That although greatly emaciated, and feeble as an infant, a decidedly healthy action had taken place, and the (sic) docter expressed confident hopes of her recovery.

"May I not see her, Mrs. Turner?" he asked, earnestly.

"Not yet, Mr. Martin, The doctor is positive in his directions to have her kept perfectly quiet."

T. S. Arthur

Martin had, of course, to acquiesce, but with great reluctance. For five days more he continued to call in twice every day, and each time found her slightly improved.

"May I not see her now?" he again asked, at the end of these additional days of anxious self-denial.

"If you will not talk to her," said Mrs. Turner.

Martin promised, and was shown up to her chamber. His heart sickened as he approached the bed-side, and looked upon the thin, white, almost expressionless face, and sunken eye, of her who was now the ruler of his affections. He took her hand, that returned a feeble, almost imperceptible pressure, but did not trust himself to utter her name. She hardly seemed conscious of his presence, and he soon turned away, sad, very sad, yet full of hope for her recovery.

The healthy action continued, and in a week Mary could bear conversation. As soon as she could begin to sit up, Martin passed every evening with her, and seeing, as he now did, with different eyes, he perceived in her a hundred things to admire that had before escaped his notice. Recovering rapidly, in a month she was fully restored to health, and looked better than she had for years.

Just about this time, as Martin was making up his mind to declare himself her lover, he was surprised, on entering their parlor one evening, to find on the table a large brass door-plate, with the words, "MARY TURNER, FANCY DRESS MAKER," engraved upon it.

"Why, what are you going to do with this Mary?" he asked, forgetting that she did not know his peculiar thoughts about her.

"I am going to commence my business," she replied in a quiet tone. "I have learned a trade, and now I must turn it, if possible, to some good account."

"But your health won't bear it, Mary," he urged. "Don't you know that you made yourself sick by your close application in learning your trade?"

"I do, Mr. Martin; but still, you know why I learned my trade."

Mr. Martin paused for a few moments, and then looking into her face, said -

"Yes, I know the reason, Mary, and I always admired your noble independence in acting as you did - nay," and he took her hand, "If you will permit me to say so, have loved you ever since I had a true appreciation of your character. May I hope for a return of kindred feelings?"

Mary Turner's face became instantly crimsoned with burning blushes, but she did not withdraw her hand. A brief silence ensued, during which the only sounds audible to the ears of each, was the beating of their own hearts. Martin at length said -

"Have I aught to hope, Mary?"

"You know, Mr. Martin," she replied, in a voice that slightly trembled, "that I have duties to perform beyond myself. However much my feelings may be interested, these cannot be set aside. Under present circumstances, my hand is not my own to give."

"But, your duties will become mine, Mary; and most gladly will I assume them. Only give me your hand, and in return I will give you a home for all you love, and you can do for them just as your heart desires. Will you now be mine?"

"If my mother object not," she said, bursting into tears.

Of course, the mother had no objection to urge, and in a few weeks they were married. It was, perhaps, three months after

T. S. Arthur

this event, that the now happy family were seated in a beautifully furnished parlor, large enough to suit even Mrs. Turner's ideas. Something had turned their thoughts on the past, and Mary alluded to their sad experience in keeping boarders.

"You did not lose much, did you?" asked her husband.

"We sunk over two thousand dollars," Mary replied.

"Is it possible! You paid rather dear, then, for your experience in keeping a boarding house."

"So I then thought," Mary answered, looking into his face with a smile, "But I believe it was money well laid out. What you call a good investment."

"How so?"

Mary stooped down to the ear of her husband, who sat a little behind her mother, and whispered,

"You are dull, dear - I got you by it, didn't I?"

His young wife's cheek was very convenient, and his lips touched it almost involuntarily.

"What is that, Mary?" asked her mother, turning towards them, for she had heard her remark, and was waiting for the explanation.

"Oh, nothing, mother, it was only some of my fun."

"You seem quite full of fun, lately," said Mrs. Turner, with a quiet smile of satisfaction, and again bent her eyes upon the book she was reading.

CHAPTER XXX

TWO WAYS WITH DOMESTICS

"AH, good morning, dear! I'm really glad to see you," said Helen Armitage to her young friend Fanny Milnor, as the latter came in to sit an hour with her. "I just wanted a little sunshine."

"There ought to be plenty of sunshine here," returned Fanny smiling. "You always seem happy, and so does your mother and sister Mary, whenever I meet you abroad."

"Abroad, or at home, makes quite a difference, Fanny. Precious little sunshine have we here. Not a day passes over our heads, that we are not thrown into hot water about something or other, with our abominable servants. I declare! I never saw the like, and it grows worse and worse every day."

"Indeed! That is bad, sure enough. But can't you remedy this defect in some way?"

"We try hard enough, dear knows! I believe we have had no less than, six cooks, and as many chambermaids in the last three months. But change only makes the matter worse. Sometimes they are so idle and dirty that we cannot tolerate them for a week. And then again they are so ill-natured, and downright saucy, that no one can venture to speak to them."

As Helen Armitage said this, she arose from her chair, and

T. S. Arthur

walking deliberately across the room, rang the parlor bell, and then quietly walked back again and resumed her seat, continuing her remarks as she did so, upon the exhaustless theme she had introduced. In a little while a domestic entered.

"That door has been left open by some one," the young lady said, in a half vexed tone of authority, and with a glance of reproof, as she pointed to the door of the back parlor leading into the passage.

The servant turned quickly away, muttering as she did so, and left the parlor, slamming the door after her with a sudden, indignant jerk.

"You see that!" remarked Helen, the color deepening on her cheeks, and her voice indicating a good deal of inward disturbance. "That's just the way we are served by nine out of ten of the people we get about us. They neglect every thing, and then, when reminded of their duty, flirt, and grumble, and fling about just as you saw that girl do this moment. I'll ring for her again, and make her shut that door as she ought to do, the insolent creature!"

Helen was rising, when Fanny laid her hand on her arm, and said, in a quiet persuasive tone,

"No - no - don't, Helen. She is out of temper, and will only retort angrily at further reproof. The better way is to pass over these things as if you did not notice them."

"And let them ride over us rough shod, as they most certainly will! The fact is, with all our efforts to make them know and keep their places, we find it impossible to gain any true subordination in the house."

"We never have any trouble of this kind," Fanny said.

"You must be very fortunate then."

"I don't know as to that. I never recollect an instance in which a domestic opposed my mother or failed to obey, cheerfully, any request. And we have had several in our house, within my recollection. At least half a dozen."

"Half a dozen! Oh, dear! We have half a dozen a month sometimes! But come, let us go up to my room; I have some new prints to show you. They are exquisite. My father bought them for me last week."

The two young ladies ascended to Helen's chamber in the third story. But the book of prints was not to be found there. "It is in the parlor, I recollect now," said Helen, ringing the bell as she spoke, with a quick, strong jerk.

In about three or four minutes, and just as the young lady's patience was exhausted and her fingers were beginning to itch for another pull at the bell rope, the tardy waiting women appeared.

"Hannah - Go down into the parlor, and bring me off of the piano a book you will find there. It is a broad flat book, with loose sheets in it."

This was said in a tone of authority. The domestic turned away without speaking and went down stairs. In a little while she came back, and handed Helen a book, answering the description given. But it was a portfolio of music.

"O no! Not this!" said she, with a curl of the lip, and an impatient tossing of her head. "How stupid you are, Hannah! The book I want, contains prints, and this is only a music book! There! Take it back, and bring me the book of prints."

Hannah took the book, and muttering as she went out, returned to the parlor, down two long flights of stairs, and laid it upon the piano.

"If you want the pictures, you may get them yourself, Miss;

you've got more time to run up and down stairs than I have."

As she said this Hannah left the parlor, and the book of prints lying upon the piano, and went back to the chamber she had been engaged in cleaning up when called away by Helen's bell. It was not long after she had resumed her occupation, before the bell sounded loudly through the passages. Hannah smiled bitterly, and with an air of resolution, as she listened to the iron summons.

"Pull away to your heart's content, Miss!" she said, half audibly. "When you call me again take care and know what you want me for. I've got something else to do besides running up and down stairs to bring you pictures. Why didn't you look at them while you were in the parlor, or, take them up with you, if you wanted them in your chamber?"

"Did you ever see the like!" ejaculated Helen, deeply disturbed at finding both her direction and her subsequent summons unattended to. "That's just the way we are constantly served by these abominable creatures."

Two or three heavy jerks at the bell rope followed these remarks.

"Pull away! It's good exercise for you!" muttered Hannah to herself. And this was all the notice she took of the incensed young lady, who was finally compelled to go down stairs and get the prints herself. But she was so much disturbed and caused Fanny to feel so unpleasantly that neither of them had any real enjoyment in examining the beautiful pictures. After these had been turned over and remarked upon for some time, and they had spent an hour in conversation, the bell was again rung. Hannah, who came with her usual reluctance, was directed to prepare some lemonade, and bring it up with cake. This she did, after a good deal of delay, for which she was grumbled at by Helen. After the cake bad been eaten, and the lemonade drank, Hannah was again summoned to remove the waiter. This was performed with the same ill grace that every other service had been rendered.

"I declare! these servants worry me almost to death!" Helen again broke forth. "This is just the way I am served whenever I have a visiter. It is always the time Hannah takes to be ill-natured and show off her disobliging, ugly temper."

Fanny made no reply to this. But she had her own thoughts. It was plain enough to her mind, that her friend had only herself to blame, for the annoyance she suffered. After witnessing one or two mote petty contentions with the domestic, Fanny went away, her friend promising, at her particular request, to come and spend a day with her early in the ensuing week.

It can do no harm, and may do good, for us to draw aside for an instant the veil that screened from general observation the domestic economy of the Armitage family. They were well enough off in the world as regards wealth, but rather poorly off in respect to self-government and that domestic wisdom which arranges all parts of a household in just subordination, and thus prevents collisions, or encroachments of one portion upon another. With them, a servant was looked upon as a machine who had nothing to do but to obey all commands. As to the rights of servants in a household, that was something of which they had never dreamed. Of course, constant rebellion, or the most unwillingly preformed duties, was the undeviating attendant upon their domestic economy. It was a maxim, with Mrs. Armitage, never to indulge or favor one of her people in the smallest matter. She had never done so in her life, she said, that she had got any thanks for it. It always made them presumptuous and dissatisfied. The more you did for them, the more they expected, and soon came to demand as a right what had been at first granted as a favor. Mrs. Armitage was, in a word, one of those petty domestic tyrants, who rule with the rod of apparent authority. Perfect submission she deemed the only true order in a household. Of course, true order she never could gain, for such a thing as perfect submission to arbitrary rule among domestics in this country never has and never will be yielded. The law of kindness and consideration is the only true law, and where this is not efficient, none other will or can be.

As for Mrs. Armitage and her daughters, each one of whom bore herself towards the domestics with an air of imperiousness and dictation, they never reflected before requiring a service whether such a service would not be felt as burdensome in the extreme, and therefore, whether it might not be dispensed with at the time. Without regard to what might be going on in the kitchen, the parlor or chamber, bells were rung, and servants required to leave their half finished meals, or to break away in the midst of important duties that had to be done by a certain time, to attend to some trifling matter which, in fact, should never have been assigned to a domestic at all. Under this system, it was no wonder that a constant succession of complaints against servants should be made by the Armitages. How could it be otherwise? Flesh and blood could not patiently bear the trials to which these people were subjected. Nor was it any wonder, that frequent changes took place, or that they were only able to retain the most inferior class of servants, and then only for short periods.

There are few, perhaps, who cannot refer, among their acquaintances, to a family like the Armitages. They may ordinarily be known by their constant complaints about servants, and their dictatorial way of speaking whenever they happen to call upon them for the performance of any duty.

In pleasing contrast to them were the Milnors.

Let us go with Helen in her visit to Fanny. When the day came which she had promised to spend with her young friend, Helen, after getting out of patience with the chambermaid for her tardy attendance upon her, and indulging her daily murmurs against servants, at last emerged into the street, and took her way towards the dwelling of Mr. Milnor. It was a bright day, and her spirits soon rose superior to the little annoyances that had fretted her for the past hour. When she met Fanny she was in the best possible humor; and so seemed the tidy domestic who had admitted her, for she looked very cheerful, and smiled as she opened the door.

"How different from our grumbling, slovenly set!" Helen could not help remarking to herself, as she passed in. Fanny welcomed her with genuine cordiality, and the two young ladies were soon engaged in pleasant conversation. After exhausting various themes. they turned to music, and played, and sang together for half an hour.

"I believe I have some new prints that you have never seen," said Fanny on their leaving the piano, and she looked around for the portfolio of engravings, but could not find it.

"Oh! now I remember - it is up stairs. Excuse me for a minute and I will run and get it." As Fanny said this, she glided from the room. In a few minutes she returned with the book of prints.

"Pardon me, Fanny - but why didn't you call a servant to get the port-folio for you? You have them in the house to wait upon you."

"Oh, as to that," returned Fanny, "I always prefer to wait upon myself when I can, and so remain independent. And besides, the girls are all busy ironing, and I would not call them off from their work for any thing that I could do myself. Ironing day is a pretty hard day for all of them, for our family is large, and mother always likes her work done well."

"But, if you adopt that system, you'll soon have them grumbling at the merest trifle you may be compelled to ask them to do."

"So far from that, Helen, I never make a request of any domestic in the house, that is not instantly and cheerfully met. To make you sensible of the good effects of the system I pursue of not asking to be waited on when I can help myself, I will mention that as I came down just now with these engravings in my hand, I met our chambermaid on the stairs, with a basket of clothes in her hands - 'There now, Miss Fanny,' she said half reprovingly, 'why didn't you call me to get that for you, and not leave your company in the parlor?' There is no reluctance about her, you see. She knows that I spare her whenever I can, and she is willing to oblige me, whenever she can do so."

"Truly, she must be the eighth wonder of the world!" said, Helen in laughing surprise. "Who ever heard of a servant that asked as a favor to be permitted to serve you? All of which I ever saw, or heard, cared only to get out of doing every thing, and strove to be as disobliging as possible."

"It is related of the good Oberlin," replied Fanny, "that he was asked one day by an old female servant who had been in his house for many years, whether there were servants in heaven. On his inquiring the reason for so singular a question, he received, in substance, this reply - 'Heaven will be no heaven to me, unless I have the privilege of ministering to your wants and comfort there as I have the privilege of doing here. I want to be your servant even in heaven.' Now why, Helen, do you suppose that faithful old servant was so strongly attached to Oberlin?"

"Because, I presume, he had been uniformly kind to her."

"No doubt that was the principal reason. And that I presume is the reason why there is no domestic in our house who will not, at any time, do for me cheerfully, and with a seeming pleasure, any thing I ask of her. I am sure I never spoke cross to one of them in my life - and I make it a point never to ask them to do for me what I can readily do for myself."

"Your mother must be very fortunate in her selection of servants. There, I presume, lies the secret. We never had one who would bear the least consideration. Indeed, ma makes it a rule on no account to grant a servant any indulgences whatever, it only spoils them, she says. You must keep them right down to it, or they soon get good for nothing."

"My mother's system is very different," Fanny said - "and we have no trouble."

The young ladies then commenced examining the prints, after which, Fanny asked to be excused a moment. In a little while she returned with a small waiter of refreshments. Helen did not remark upon this, and Fanny made no allusion to the fact of not having called a servant from the kitchen to do what she could so easily do herself. A book next engaged their attention, and occupied them until dinner time. At the stable, a tidy domestic waited with cheerful alacrity, so different from the sulky, slow attendance, at home.

"Some water, Rachael, if you please." Or, "Rachael, step down and, bring up some hot potatoes." Or - "Here, Rachael," with a pleasant smile, "you have forgotten the salt spoons," were forms of addressing a waiter upon the table so different from what Helen had ever heard, that she listened to them with utter amazement. And she was no less surprised to see with what cheerful alacrity every direction, or rather request, was obeyed.

After they all rose from the table, and had retired to the parlor, a pleasant conversation took place, in which no allusions whatever were made to the dreadful annoyance of servants, an almost unvarying subject of discourse at Mr. Armitage's, after the conclusion of nearly every badly cooked, illy served meal. - A discourse too often overheard by some one of the domestics and retailed in the kitchen, to breed confirmed ill-will, and a spirit of opposition towards the principal members of the family.

Nearly half an hour had passed from the time they had risen from the table, when a younger sister of Fanny's, who was going out to a little afternoon party, asked if Rachael might not be called up from the kitchen to get something for her.

T. S. Arthur

"No, my dear, not until she has finished her dinner," was the mild reply of Mrs. Milnor.

"But it won't take her over a minute, mother, and I am in a hurry."

"I can't help it, my dear. You will have to wait. Rachael must not be disturbed at her meals. You should have thought of this before, dinner. You know I have always tried to impress upon your mind, that there are certain hours in which domestics must not be called upon to do any thing, unless of serious importance. They have their rights, as well, as we have, and it is just as wrong for us to encroach upon their rights, as it is for them to encroach upon ours."

"Never mind, mother, I will wait," the little girl said, cheerfully. "But I thought, it was such a trifle, and would have taken her only a minute."

"It is true, my dear, that is but a trifle. Still, even trifles of this kind we should form the habit of avoiding; for they may seriously annoy at a time when we dream not that they are thought of for a moment. Think how, just as you had seated yourself at the table, tired and hungry, you would like to be called away, your food scarcely tasted, to perform some task, the urgency of which to you, at least, was very questionable?"

"I was wrong I know, mother," the child replied, "and you are right."

All this was new and strange doctrine to Helen Armitage, but she was enabled to see, from the manner in which Mrs. Milnor represented the subject, that it was true doctrine. As this became clear to her mind, she saw with painful distinctness the error that had thrown disorder into every part of her mother's household; and more than this, she inwardly resolved, that, so far as her action was concerned, a new order of things should take place. In this she was in earnest - so much so, that she made some allusion to the difference of things at home, to what they were at Mrs. Milnor's, and frankly confessed that she had not acted upon the kind and considerate principles that seemed to govern all in this well-ordered family.

"My dear child!" Mrs. Milnor said to her, with affectionate earnestness, in reply to this allusion - "depend upon it, four-fifths of the bad domestics are made so by injudicious treatment. They are, for the most part, ignorant of almost every thing, and too often, particularly, of their duties in a family. Instead of being borne with, instructed, and treated with consideration, they are scolded, driven and found fault with. Kind words they too rarely receive; and no one can well and cheerfully perform all that is required of her as a domestic, if she is never spoken to kindly, never considered - never borne with, patiently. It is in our power to make a great deal of work for our servants that is altogether unnecessary - and of course, in our power to save them many steps, and many moments of time. If we are in the chambers, and wish a servant for any thing, and she is down in the kitchen engaged, it is always well to think twice before we ring for her once. It may be, that we do not really want the attendance of any one, or can just as well wait until some errand has brought her up stairs. Then, there are various little things in which we can help ourselves and ought to do it. It is unpardonable, I think, for a lady to ring for a servant to come up one or two pairs of stairs merely to hand her a drink, when all she has to do is to cross the room, and get it for herself. Or for a young lady to require a servant to attend to all her little wants, when she can and ought to help herself, even if it takes her from the third story to the kitchen, half a dozen times a day. Above all, domestics should never be scolded. If reproof is necessary, let it be administered in a calm mild voice, and the reasons shown why the act complained of is wrong. This is the only way in which any good is done."

"I wish my mother could only learn that," said Helen, mentally, as Mrs. Milnor ceased speaking. When she returned home, it was with a deeply formed resolution never again to speak reprovingly to any of her mother's domestics - never to order them to do any thing for her, - and never to require them to wait upon her when she could just as well help herself. In this she proved firm. The consequence was, an entire change in Hannah's deportment towards her, and a cheerful performance by her of every thing she asked her to do. This could not but be observed by her mother, and it induced her to modify, to some extent, her way of treating her servants. The result was salutary, and now she has far less trouble with them than she ever had in her life. All, she finds, are not so worthless as she had deemed them.

CHAPTER XXXI

A MOTHER'S DUTY

I CLOSE my volume of rambling sketches, with a chapter more didactic and serious. The duties of the housekeeper and mother, usually unite in the same person; but difficult and perplexing as is the former relation, how light and easy are all its claims compared with those of the latter. Among my readers are many mothers - Let us for a little while hold counsel together.

To the mind of a mother, who loves her children, no subject can have so deep an interest as that which has respect to the well being of her offspring. Young mothers, especially, feel the need, the great need of the hints and helps to be derived from others' experience. To them, the duty of rightly guiding, forming and developing the young mind is altogether a new one; at every step they feel their incompetence, and are troubled at their want of success. A young married friend, the mother of two active little boys, said to me, one day, earnestly,

"Oh! I think, sometimes, that I would give the world if I only could see clearly what was my duty towards my children. I try to guide them aright - I try to keep them from all improper influences - but rank weeds continually spring up with the flowers I have planted. How shall I extirpate these, without injuring the others?"

How many a young mother thus thinks and feels. It is indeed a

T. S. Arthur

great responsibility that rests upon her. With the most constant and careful attention, she will find the task of keeping out the weeds a hard one; but let her not become weary or discouraged. The enemy is ever seeking to sow tares amid her wheat, and he will do it if she sleep at her post. Constant care, good precept, and, above all, good example, will do much. The gardener whose eye is ever over, and whose hand is ever busy in his garden, accomplishes much; the measure of his success may be seen if the eye rest for but a moment on the garden of his neighbor, the sluggard. Even if a weed springs here and there, it is quickly plucked up, and never suffered to obstruct or weaken the growth of esculent plants. A mole may enter stealthily, marring the beauty of a flower-bed, and disturbing the roots of some garden-favorite, but through the careful husbandman's well set enclosure, no beasts find an entrance. So it will be with the watchful, conscientious mother. She will so fence around her children from external dangers and allurements, that destructive beasts will be kept out; and she will, at the same time cultivate the garden of their good affections, and extirpate the weeds, that her children may grow up in moral health and beauty.

All this can be done. But the right path must be seen before we can walk in it. Every mother feels as the one I have alluded to; but some, while they feel as deeply, have not the clear perceptions of what is right that others have. Much has been written on the subject of guiding and governing children - much that is good, and much that is of doubtful utility. I will here present, from the pen of an English lady, whose work has not, we believe, been re-printed in this country, a most excellent series of precepts. They deserve to be written in letters of gold, and hung up in every nursery. She says -

"The moment a child is born into the world, a mother's duties commence; and of all those which God has allotted to mortals, there are none so important as those which devolve upon a mother.

More feeble and helpless than any thing else of living creatures is an infant in the first days of its existence - unable to minister to its own wants, unable even to make those wants known: a feeble cry which indicates suffering, but not what or where the pain is, is all it can utter. But to meet this weakness and incapacity on the part of the infant, God has implanted in the heart of the mother a yearning affection to her offspring, so that she feels this almost inanimate being to be a part of herself, and every cry of pain acts as a dagger to her own heart.

And to humanity alone, of all the tribes of animated beings, has a power been given to nullify this feeling. Beast, bird, and insect, attend to the wants of their offspring, accordingly as those wants require much or little assiduity. But woman, if she will, can drug and stupefy this feeling. She can commit the charge of her child to dependants and servants, and need only to take care that enough is provided to meet that child's wants, but need not see herself that those wants are actually met.

But a woman who does this is far, very far, from doing her duty. Who is so fit to watch over the wants of infancy as she who gave that infant birth? Can a mother suppose, that if she can so stifle those sensibilities which prompt her to provide for the wants of her children, servants and dependants, in whom no such sensibilities exist, will be very solicitous about their charge? How many of the infant's cries will be unattended to, which would at once have made their way to the heart of a mother! and, therefore, how many of the child's wants will in consequence remain uncared for!

No one can understand so well the wants of a child as a mother - no one is ever so ready to meet those wants as she; and, therefore, to none but a mother, under ordinary circumstances, should the entire charge of a child be committed, And in all countries in which, luxury has not so far attained the ascendency, that in order to partake of its pleasures a mother will desert her offspring, the cares and trials of maternal love are entered upon as the sweetest of enjoyments and the greatest of pleasures. It was a noble saying of a queen of France, "that none should share with her the privileges of a mother;" and if the same sentiment found its way into every heart, a very different aspect would soon be produced. How many, through ill-treatment and neglect in childhood, carry the marks to their dying day in weak and sickly constitutions! how many more in a distorted body and crippled limbs! These are but the too sure consequences of the neglect of a mother, and, consequent upon that, the neglect of servants, who, feeling the child a burden, lessen their own trouble; and many a mother who, perhaps, now that her child has grown up, weeps bitter tears over his infirmities, might have saved his pain and her own sorrow by attending to his wants in infancy.

"Can a mother forget her sucking child?" asks the inspired penman, in a way that it would seem to be so great an anomaly as almost to amount to an impossibility. Yet modern luxury not only proves that such a thing can be done, but it is one even of common occurrence. But if done, surely some great stake must be pending - something on which life and property are concerned - that a mother can thus forget the child of her bosom? Alas! no; the child is neglected, that no interruption may take place in the mother's stream of pleasure. For the blandishments of the theatre, or the excitements of the dance, is a child left to the charge of those who have nothing of love for it - no sympathy for its sufferings, no joyousness in sharing in its pleasures.

A woman forfeits all claim to the sacred character of a mother if she abandon her offspring to the entire care of others: for ere she can do this, she must have stifled all the best feelings of her nature, and become "worse than the infidel" - for she gives freely to the stranger, and neglects her own.

Therefore should a woman, if she would fulfil her duty, make her child her first care. It is not necessary that her whole time should be spent in attending to its wants; but it is necessary that so much of the time should be spent, that nothing should be neglected which could add to the child's comfort and happiness. And not only is it needful that a woman should show a motherly fondness for her child, so that she should attend to its wants and be solicitous for its welfare; it is also necessary that she should know how those wants are best to be provided for, and how that welfare is best to be consulted: for to the natural feelings which prompt animals to provide for their offspring, to humanity is added the noble gift of reason; so that thought and solicitude are not merely the effects of blind instinct, but the produce of a higher and nobler faculty.

As we have already adverted to this point, we shall only say, that without a knowledge of how the physical wants of a child are to be met in the best manner, a mother cannot be said to be performing her duty; for the kindness which is bestowed may be but the result of natural feeling, which it would be far harder to resist than to fulfil; whereas the want of knowledge may have resulted from ignorance and idleness, and the loss of this knowledge will never be made up by natural kindness and love: it will be like trying to work without hands, or to see when the eyes are blinded.

But there is yet a higher duty devolving upon woman. She has to attend to the mental and moral wants of her offspring, as well as to the physical. And helpless as we are born into the world if reference be made to our physical wants, we are yet more helpless if reference be made to our mental and moral. We come into the world with evil passions, perverted faculties, and unholy dispositions: for let what will be said of the blandness and attractiveness of children, there are in those young hearts the seeds of evil; and it needs but that a note be taken of what passes in the every-day life of a child, to convince that all is not so amiable as at first sight appears, but that the heart hides dark deformity, headstrong passions, and vicious thoughts. And to a mother's lot it falls to be the instructress of her children - their guide and pattern, and she fails in her duty when she fails in either of these points. But it may be said, that the requirement is greater than humanity can perform, and that it would need angelic purity to be able fully to meet it; for who shall say that she is so perfect that no inconsistencies shall appear between what she teaches and what she practises?

It would be, indeed, to suppose mothers more than human to think that their instructions should be perfect. The best of mothers are liable to err, and the love a mother has for her child may tempt her frequently to pass over faults which she knows ought to be corrected. But making due allowance for human incompetency and human weakness, still will a mother be bound to the utmost of her power to be the instructress of her child, equally by the lesson she inculcates and the pattern she exhibits.

There is, indeed, too much neglect shown in the instruction of children. Mothers seem to think, that if amiable qualities are shown in the exterior, no instruction is necessary for the heart. But this is a most futile attempt to make children virtuous; it is like attempting to purify water half-way down the stream, and leaving it still foul at the source. The heart should be the first thing instructed; a motive and a reason should be given for every requirement - a motive and a reason should be given for every abstinence called for - and when the heart is made to love virtue, the actions will be those of virtue; for it is the heart which is the great mover of all actions - and the moment a child can distinguish between a smile and a frown, from that moment should instruction commence - an instruction suited indeed to infantine capacities, but which should be enlarged as the child's capacities expand. It is very bad policy to suffer the first years of a child's life to pass without instruction; for if good be not written on the mind, there is sure to be evil. It is a mother's duty to watch the expanding intellect of her child, and to suit her instructions accordingly: it is equally so to learn its disposition - to study its wishes, its hopes and its fears, and to direct, control, and point them to noble aims and ends.

Oh! not alone is it needful that a mother be solicitous for the health and happiness of her child on earth: a far higher and more important thought should engage her attention - concern for her child as an immortal and an accountable being.

To all who bear the endearing name of mother, thus would we speak:

That child with whom you are so fondly playing - whose happy and smiling (sic) contenance might serve for the representation of a cherub, and whose merry laugh rings joyously and free - yes! That blooming child, notwithstanding all these pleasing and attractive smiles, has a heart prone to evil. To you is it committed to be the teacher of that child; and on that teaching will mainly if not entirely depend its future happiness or misery; not of a few brief years - not of a lifetime, but of eternity; for though a dying creature, it is still immortal, and the happiness or misery of that immortality depends upon your instruction.

Will you neglect or refuse to be your child's teacher? Shall the world and its pleasures draw off your attention from your duty when so much is at stake? or, will you leave your child to glean knowledge as best it can, thus imbibing all principles and all habits, most of them unwholesome, and many poisonous? You can decide - you, the mother. You gave it life, you may make that life a blessing or a curse, as you (sic) inclulcate good or evil; for if through your neglect, or through bad example, you let evil passions obtain an ascendency, that child may grow into a dissolute and immoral man; his career may be one of debauchery and profaneness; and then, when he comes to die, in the agonies of remorse, in the delirium of a conscience-stricken spirit, he may gasp out his last breath with a curse on your head, for having given him life, but not a disposition to use it aright, so that his has been a life of shame and disgrace here, and will be one of misery hereafter. That child's character is yet untainted; with you that decision rests - his destiny is in your hands. He may have dispositions the most dark and foul - falseness, hatred and revenge; but you may prevent their growth. He may have dispositions the most bland and attractive; you can so order it that contact with the world shall never sully them. Yes, you - the mother - can prevent the evil and nurture the good. You can teach that child - you can rear it, discipline it. You can make your offspring so love you, that the memory of your piety shall prevent their wickedness, and the hallowed recollection of your goodness stimulate their own.

And equally in your power is it to neglect your child. By suffering pleasure to lure you - by following the follies of fashion, or by the charm of those baubles which the world presents to the eye, but keeps from your grasp - you may neglect your child. But you have neglected a plain and positive duty - a duty which is engraven on your heart and wound into your nature: and a duty neglected is sure, sooner or later, to come back again as an avenger to punish; while, on the other hand, a duty performed to the best of the ability returns back to the performer laden with a blessing.

But it may be said, how are children to be trained in order that happiness may be the result?

It is quite impossible to lay down rules for the management of children; since those which would serve for guidance in regulating the conduct of one child, would work the worst results when applied to another. But we mention a few particulars.

The grand secret in the management of children is to treat them as reasonable beings. We see that they are governed by hope, fear, and love: these feelings, then, should be made the instruments by which their education is conducted. Whenever it is possible (and it is very rarely that it is not), a reason should be given for every requirement, and a motive for the undertaking any task: this would lead the child to see that nothing was demanded out of caprice or whim, but that it was a requirement involving happiness as well as duty.

This method would also teach the child to reverence and respect the parent. She would be regarded as possessed of superior knowledge; and he would the more readily undertake demands for which he could see no reason, from a knowledge that no commands of which he understood the design were ever unreasonable.

The manner of behaving to children should be one of kindness, though marked by decision of character. An over fondness should never allow a mother to gratify her child in any thing unreasonable; and after having once refused a request - which she should not do hastily or unadvisedly - no coaxing or tears should divert her from her purpose; for if she gives way, the child will at once understand that he has a power over his mother, and will resort to the same expedient whenever occasion may require; and a worse evil than this is, that respect for the parent will be lost, and the child, in place of yielding readily to her wishes, will try means of trick and evasion to elude them.

In order to really manage a child well, a mother should become a child herself; she should enter into its hopes and fears, and share its joys and sorrows; she should bend down her mind to that of her offspring, so as to be pleased with all those trivial actions which give it pleasure, and to sorrow over those which bring it pain. This would secure a love firm and ardent, and at the same time lasting; for as a child advanced in strength of intellect, so might the mother, until the child grew old enough to understand the ties which bound them; and then, by making him a friend, she would bind him to her for life.

There are none of the human race so sagacious and (sic) keensighed as children: they seem to understand intuitively a person's disposition, and they quickly notice any discrepancies or inconsistencies of conduct. On this point should particular attention be paid, that there be nothing practised to cheat the child. Underhand means are frequently resorted to, to persuade a child to perform or abstain from some particular duty or object; but in a very short time it will be found out, and the child has been taught a lesson in deception which it will not fail to use when occasion requires.

And under this head might be included all that petty species of deceit used towards children, whether to mislead their apprehension, or to divert their attention. If any thing be improper for a child to know or do, better tell him so at once, than resort to an underhand expedient. If a reason can be given for requiring the abstinence; it should; but if not tell the child that the reason is such that he could not comprehend it, and he will remain satisfied. But if trick or scheming be resorted to, the child will have learned the two improper lessons of first being cunning, and then telling a falsehood to avoid it.

In whatever way you wish to act upon a child, always propose the highest and noblest motive - this will generally be a motive which centres in God. Thus, in teaching a child to speak the truth, it should be proposed not so much out of obedience to parents, as out of obedience to God; and in all requirements the love and fear of God should be prominently set forth.

A child is born with feelings of religion; and if these feelings are properly called forth, the actions will generally have a tendency to good. Thus, with a child whose disposition is to deceive, a mother has no hold upon such an one; for the child will soon perceive that his mother cannot follow him every where, and that he can commit with impunity many actions of deceit. But, impress the child with the truth that a Being is watching these actions, and that though done with the greatest cunning, they cannot be committed with impunity, and it is more than probable that they will never be committed at all. A temptation may be thrown in the way of such a child, but it will not be powerful enough to overcome the feeling that the action is watched. That child may eagerly pant to perform the forbidden action, or to partake of the forbidden pleasure; but he will not be able to rid himself of the feeling that it cannot be done without being observed. He will stand in a state of anxiety, and steal a glance around, in order to see the Being he feels is looking upon him, and every breeze that murmurs will be a voice to chide him, and every leaf that whistles will seem a footstep, and never will he be able to break the restraint; for wherever he goes and whatever he does, he will feel that his actions are watched by one who will punish the bad and reward the good.

And in the same way might this be applied to all dispositions and feelings. How cheering is it to a timid child to be told that at no time is he left alone: but that the Being who made every thing preserves and keeps every thing, and that nothing can happen but by his permission! This is to disarm fear of its terrors, and toimplant a confidence in the mind, for the child will feel that while his actions are good he is under the protection of an Almighty Parent. In the same way, in stimulating a child to the performance of a duty, the end proposed should be the favour of God. This would insure the duty being entered upon with a right spirit - not merely for the sake of show and effect, but springing from the heart and the mind - and, at the same time, it would prevent any thing of hypocrisy. If it were only the estimation of the world which was to be regarded, a child could soon understand that the applause would be gained by the mere exterior performance, be the motive what it might: but when the motive is centered in God, it is readily understood that the feeling must be genuine; otherwise, whatever the world may say, God will look upon it as unworthy and base. We believe it would be found to work the best results, if all the actions of a child were made thus to depend upon their harmony with the will of God; for it would give a sacredness to every action, make every motive a high and holy one, and harmonise the thoughts of the heart with the actions of the life.

But in this mode of teaching, it is essentially necessary that a mother should herself be an example of the truth she teaches. It will be worse than useless to teach a child that God is always at hand, 'and spieth out all our ways,' if she act as though she did not believe in the existence of a Deity.

In the same way will it hold good of every requirement. It will be vain to teach a child that lying is a great crime in God's sight, when a mother in her own words sho s no regard to truth; and equally so of all other passions and feelings. It is idle to teach a child that pride - hatred - revenge - anger, are unholy passions, if a mother's own conduct displays either of them. How useless is it to teach that vanity should never be indulged in, when a mother delights in display! Such instruction as this is like the web of Penelope - unpicked as fast as done. The greatest reverence is due to a child; and previously to becoming a teacher, a mother should learn this hardest of all lessons - 'Know thyself.' Without this, the instruction she gives her children will at best prove very imperfect. It is quite useless to teach children to reverence any thing, when a mother's conduct shows that, practically at least, she has no belief in the truths she inculcates. And a very hard requirement this is: but it is a requirement absolutely necessary, if education is meant to be any thing more than nominal. The finest lesson on the beauty of truth is enforced by a mother never herself saying what is false; for children pay great regard to consistency, and very soon detect any discrepancies between that which is taught and that which is practised.

The best method of inculcating truth on the minds of children is by analogy and illustration. They cannot follow an argument, though they readily understand a comparison: and, by a judicious arrangement, every thing, either animate or inanimate, might be made to become a teacher. What lesson on industry would be so likely to be instructive as that gathered from a bee-hive? The longest dissertation on the evils of idleness and the advantages of industry would not prove half so beneficial as directing the observation to the movements of the bee - that ever-active insect, which, without the aid of reason, exercises prudence and foresight, and provides against the wants of winter. A child will readily understand such instruction as this, and will blush to be found spending precious hours in idleness. And in the same way with other duties, whether to God or mankind, the fowls of the air and the flowers of the field might be made profitable teachers, and the child would, wherever he went, be (sic) surronded with instruction.

This mode of teaching has this special recommendation - it raises up no evil passions: and a child which would display an evil temper by being reproved in words, will feel no such rancor at a lesson being inculcated in a way like this.

This instruction will also be much longer remembered than one delivered in words, forasmuch as the object upon which the instruction is based would be continually presented to the eye.

And, we believe, almost all duties might be inculcated in this manner. Thus, humility by the lily, patience by the spider, affection by the dove, love to parents by the stork, - all might be rendered teachers, and in a way never to be forgotten. And that this mode of teaching is the best, we have the example of Christ himself, who almost invariably enforced his instructions by an allusion to some created thing. What, for instance, was so likely to teach men dependence upon God as a reference to the 'ravens and the lilies,' which without the aid of reason had their wants cared for? And in the same way with children - what is so likely to teach them their duties, as a reference to the varied things in nature with whose uses and habits they are well acquainted?

God should be the object upon which the child's thoughts are taught to dwell - for the minds even of children turn to the beautiful, and the beautiful is the Divine. All thoughts and actions should be raised to this standard; and the child would raise above the feelings of self-gratification and vanity, and the panting for applause, to the favor and love of God. Thus should religion be the great and the first thing taught; and a mother should be careful that neither in her own actions, nor in the motives she holds out to her children, should there be any thing inimical or contrary to religion.

And by this course the best and happiest results may be expected to follow. The perverse and headstrong passions of the human heart are so many, that numerous instructions may seem to be useless, and a mother may have often to sigh over her child as she sees him allowing evil habits to obtain the mastery, or unholy dispositions to reign in his heart; but, as we have before said, we do not think that the instruction will be lost, but that a time will come when she will reap the fruits of her toil, care and anxiety.

Such then is the duty of woman as a mother - to tend and watch over the wants of her child, to guard it in health, to nurse it in sickness, to be solicitous for it in all the changes of life, and to prevent, as much as possible, those many ills to which flesh is heir from assailing her fondly cherished offspring.

It is also her province to instruct her children in those duties which will fall to their lot both as reasonable and as immortal creatures; and by so doing she will make her own life happy – leave to her children a happy heritage on earth, and a prospect of a higher one in heaven. But if a mother neglect her duty, she will reap the fruits of her own negligence in the ingratitude of her children - an ingratitude which will bring a double pain to her, from the thought that her own neglect was the cause of its growth, as an eagle with an arrow in his heart might be supposed to feel an agony above that of pain on seeing the shaft now draining its life's blood feathered from its own wing.

Mrs. Child, in her excellent "Mother's Book," a volume that should be in the hands of every woman who has assumed the responsibilities of a parent, gives some valuable (sic) sugestions on the subject of governing children. I make a single extract and with it close my present rambling work. She says:

"Some children, from errors in early management, get possessed with the idea that they may have every thing. They even tease for things it would be impossible to give them. A child properly managed will seldom ask twice for what you have once told him he should not have. But if you have the care of one who has acquired this habit, the best way to cure him of it is never to give him what he asks for, whether his request is proper or not; but at the same time be careful to give him such things as he likes, (provided they are proper for him,) when he does not ask for them. This will soon break him of the habit of teasing.

"I have said much in praise of gentleness. I cannot say too much. Its effects are beyond calculation, both on the affections and the understanding. The victims of oppression and abuse are generally stupid, as well as selfish and hard-hearted. How can we wonder at it? They are all the time excited to evil passions, and nobody encourages what is good in them. We might as well expect flowers to grow amid the cold and storm of winter.

"But gentleness, important as it is, is not all that is required in education. There should be united with it firmness - great firmness. Commands should be reasonable, and given in perfect kindness; but once given, it should be known that they must be obeyed. I heard a lady once say, 'For my part, I cannot be so very strict with my children. I love them too much to punish them every time they disobey me.' I will relate a scene which took place in her family. She had but one domestic, and at the time to which I allude, she was very busy preparing for company. Her children knew by experience that when she was in a hurry she would indulge them in any thing for the sake of having them out of the way. George began, 'Mother, I want a piece of mince-pie.' The answer was, 'It is nearly bed-time; and mince-pie will hurt you. You shall have a piece of cake, if you will sit down and be still.' The boy ate his cake; and liking the system of being hired to sit still, he soon began again, 'Mother, I want a piece of mince-pie.' The old answer was repeated. The child stood his ground, 'Mother, I want a piece of mince-pie - I _want_ a piece - I _want_ a piece,' was repeated incessantly. 'Will you leave off teasing, If I give you a piece?' 'Yes, I will - certain true,' A small piece was given, and soon devoured. With his mouth half full, he began again, 'I want another piece - I want another piece.' 'No, George; I shall not give you another mouthful. Go sit down, you naughty boy. You always act the worst when I am going to have company.' George continued his teasing; and at last said, 'If you don't give me another piece, I'll roar.' This threat not being attended to, he kept his word. Upon this, the mother seized him by the shoulder, shook him angrily, saying, 'Hold your tongue, you naughty boy!' 'I will if you will give me another piece of pie,'

T. S. Arthur

said he. Another small piece was given him, after he had promised that he certainly would not tease any more. As soon as he had eaten it, he, of course, began again; and with the additional threat, 'If you don't give me a piece, I will roar after the company comes, so loud that they can all hear me.' The end of all this was, that the boy had a sound whipping, was put to bed, and could not sleep all night, because the mince-pie made his stomach ache. What an accumulation of evils in this little scene! His health injured - his promises broken with impunity - his mother's promises broken - the knowledge gained that he could always vex her when she was in a hurry - and that he could gain what he would by teasing. He always acted upon the same plan afterward; for he only once in a while (when he made his mother very angry) got a whipping; but he was *always* sure to obtain what he asked for, if he teased her long enough. His mother told him the plain truth, when she said the mince-pie would hurt him; but he did not know whether it was the truth, or whether she only said it to put him off; for he knew that she did sometimes deceive. When she gave him the pie, he had reason to suppose it was not true it would hurt him - else why should a kind mother give it to her child? Had she told him that if he asked a second time, she would put him to bed directly - and had she kept her promise, in spite of entreaties - she would have saved him a whipping, and herself a great deal of unnecessary trouble. And who can calculate all the whippings, and all the trouble, she would have spared herself and him? I do not remember ever being in her house half a day without witnessing some scene of contention with the children.

"Now let me introduce you to another acquaintance. She was in precisely the same situation, having a comfortable income and one domestic; but her children were much more numerous, and she had had very limited advantages for education. Yet she managed her family better than any woman I ever saw, or ever expect to see again. I will relate a scene I witnessed there, by way of contrast to the one I have just described. Myself and several friends once entered her parlor unexpectedly, just as the family were seated at the supper-table.

A little girl, about four years old, was obliged to be removed, to make room for us. Her mother assured her she should have her supper in a little while, if she was a good girl. The child cried; and the guests insisted that room should be made for her at table. 'No,' said the mother; 'I have told her she must wait; and if she cries, I shall be obliged to send her to bed. If she is a good little girl, she shall have her supper directly.' The child could not make up her mind to obey; and her mother led her out of the room, and gave orders that she should be put to bed without supper. When my friend returned, her husband said, 'Hannah, that was a hard case. The poor child lost her supper, and was agitated by the presence of strangers. I could hardly keep from taking her on my knee, and giving her some supper. Poor little thing! But I never will interfere with your management; and much as it went against my feelings, I entirely approve of what you have done.' 'It cost me a struggle,' replied his wife; 'but I know it is for the good of the child to be taught that I mean exactly what I say.'

"This family was the most harmonious, affectionate, happy family I ever knew. The children were managed as easily as a flock of lambs. After a few unsuccessful attempts at disobedience, when very young, they gave it up entirely; and always cheerfully acted from the conviction that their mother knew best. This family was governed with great strictness; firmness was united with gentleness. The indulgent mother, who said she loved her children too much to punish them, was actually obliged to punish them ten times as much as the strict mother did."

T. S. Arthur

Choose from Thousands of 1stWorldLibrary Classics By

A. M. Barnard
Ada Leverson
Adolphus William Ward
Aesop
Agatha Christie
Alexander Aaronsohn
Alexander Kielland
Alexandre Dumas
Alfred Gatty
Alfred Ollivant
Alice Duer Miller
Alice Turner Curtis
Alice Dunbar
Allen Chapman
Ambrose Bierce
Amelia E. Barr
Amory H. Bradford
Andrew Lang
Andrew McFarland Davis
Andy Adams
Anna Alice Chapin
Anna Sewell
Annie Besant
Annie Hamilton Donnell
Annie Payson Call
Annie Roe Carr
Annonaymous
Anton Chekhov
Arnold Bennett
Arthur Conan Doyle
Arthur M. Winfield
Arthur Ransome
Arthur Schnitzler
Atticus
B.H. Baden-Powell
B. M. Bower
B. C. Chatterjee
Baroness Emmuska Orczy
Baroness Orczy
Basil King
Bayard Taylor
Ben Macomber
Bertha Muzzy Bower
Bjornstjerne Bjornson
Booth Tarkington
Boyd Cable
Bram Stoker
C. Collodi
C. E. Orr

C. M. Ingleby
Carolyn Wells
Catherine Parr Traill
Charles A. Eastman
Charles Amory Beach
Charles Dickens
Charles Dudley Warner
Charles Farrar Browne
Charles Ives
Charles Kingsley
Charles Klein
Charles Hanson Towne
Charles Lathrop Pack
Charles Romyn Dake
Charles Whibley
Charles Willing Beale
Charlotte M. Braeme
Charlotte M. Yonge
Charlotte Perkins Stetson
Clair W. Hayes
Clarence Day Jr.
Clarence E. Mulford
Clemence Housman
Confucius
Coningsby Dawson
Cornelis DeWitt Wilcox
Cyril Burleigh
D. H. Lawrence
Daniel Defoe
David Garnett
Dinah Craik
Don Carlos Janes
Donald Keyhoe
Dorothy Kilner
Dougan Clark
Douglas Fairbanks
E. Nesbit
E.P.Roe
E. Phillips Oppenheim
Earl Barnes
Edgar Rice Burroughs
Edith Van Dyne
Edith Wharton
Edward Everett Hale
Edward J. O'Brien
Edward S. Ellis
Edwin L. Arnold
Eleanor Atkins
Eliot Gregory

Elizabeth Gaskell
Elizabeth McCracken
Elizabeth Von Arnim
Ellem Key
Emerson Hough
Emilie F. Carlen
Emily Dickinson
Enid Bagnold
Enilor Macartney Lane
Erasmus W. Jones
Ernie Howard Pie
Ethel May Dell
Ethel Turner
Ethel Watts Mumford
Eugenie Foa
Eugene Wood
Eustace Hale Ball
Evelyn Everett-green
Everard Cotes
F. H. Cheley
F. J. Cross
F. Marion Crawford
Federick Austin Ogg
Ferdinand Ossendowski
Francis Bacon
Francis Darwin
Frances Hodgson Burnett
Frances Parkinson Keyes
Frank Gee Patchin
Frank Harris
Frank Jewett Mather
Frank L. Packard
Frank V. Webster
Frederic Stewart Isham
Frederick Trevor Hill
Frederick Winslow Taylor
Friedrich Kerst
Friedrich Nietzsche
Fyodor Dostoyevsky
G.A. Henty
G.K. Chesterton
Gabrielle E. Jackson
Garrett P. Serviss
Gaston Leroux
George A. Warren
George Ade
Geroge Bernard Shaw
George Durston
George Ebers

George Eliot
George Gissing
George MacDonald
George Meredith
George Orwell
George Sylvester Viereck
George Tucker
George W. Cable
George Wharton James
Gertrude Atherton
Gordon Casserly
Grace E. King
Grace Gallatin
Grace Greenwood
Grant Allen
Guillermo A. Sherwell
Gulielma Zollinger
Gustav Flaubert
H. A. Cody
H. B. Irving
H.C. Bailey
H. G. Wells
H. H. Munro
H. Irving Hancock
H. Rider Haggard
H. W. C. Davis
Haldeman Julius
Hall Caine
Hamilton Wright Mabie
Hans Christian Andersen
Harold Avery
Harold McGrath
Harriet Beecher Stowe
Harry Castlemon
Harry Coghill
Harry Houidini
Hayden Carruth
Helent Hunt Jackson
Helen Nicolay
Hendrik Conscience
Hendy David Thoreau
Henri Barbusse
Henrik Ibsen
Henry Adams
Henry Ford
Henry Frost
Henry James
Henry Jones Ford
Henry Seton Merriman
Henry W Longfellow
Herbert A. Giles

Herbert Carter
Herbert N. Casson
Herman Hesse
Hildegard G. Frey
Homer
Honore De Balzac
Horace B. Day
Horace Walpole
Horatio Alger Jr.
Howard Pyle
Howard R. Garis
Hugh Lofting
Hugh Walpole
Humphry Ward
Ian Maclaren
Inez Haynes Gillmore
Irving Bacheller
Isabel Hornibrook
Israel Abrahams
Ivan Turgenev
J.G.Austin
J. Henri Fabre
J. M. Barrie
J. Macdonald Oxley
J. S. Fletcher
J. S. Knowles
J. Storer Clouston
Jack London
Jacob Abbott
James Allen
James Andrews
James Baldwin
James Branch Cabell
James DeMille
James Joyce
James Lane Allen
James Lane Allen
James Oliver Curwood
James Oppenheim
James Otis
James R. Driscoll
Jane Austen
Jane L. Stewart
Janet Aldridge
Jens Peter Jacobsen
Jerome K. Jerome
John Burroughs
John Cournos
John F. Kennedy
John Gay
John Glasworthy

John Habberton
John Joy Bell
John Kendrick Bangs
John Milton
John Philip Sousa
Jonas Lauritz Idemil Lie
Jonathan Swift
Joseph A. Altsheler
Joseph Carey
Joseph Conrad
Joseph E. Badger Jr
Joseph Hergesheimer
Joseph Jacobs
Jules Vernes
Julian Hawthrone
Julie A Lippmann
Justin Huntly McCarthy
Kakuzo Okakura
Kenneth Grahame
Kenneth McGaffey
Kate Langley Bosher
Kate Langley Bosher
Katherine Cecil Thurston
Katherine Stokes
L. A. Abbot
L. T. Meade
L. Frank Baum
Latta Griswold
Laura Dent Crane
Laura Lee Hope
Laurence Housman
Lawrence Beasley
Leo Tolstoy
Leonid Andreyev
Lewis Carroll
Lewis Sperry Chafer
Lilian Bell
Lloyd Osbourne
Louis Hughes
Louis Tracy
Louisa May Alcott
Lucy Fitch Perkins
Lucy Maud Montgomery
Luther Benson
Lydia Miller Middleton
Lyndon Orr
M. Corvus
M. H. Adams
Margaret E. Sangster
Margret Howth
Margaret Vandercook

Margret Penrose
Maria Edgeworth
Maria Thompson Daviess
Mariano Azuela
Marion Polk Angellotti
Mark Overton
Mark Twain
Mary Austin
Mary Catherine Crowley
Mary Cole
Mary Hastings Bradley
Mary Roberts Rinehart
Mary Rowlandson
M. Wollstonecraft Shelley
Maud Lindsay
Max Beerbohm
Myra Kelly
Nathaniel Hawthrone
Nicolo Machiavelli
O. F. Walton
Oscar Wilde
Owen Johnson
P.G. Wodehouse
Paul and Mabel Thorne
Paul G. Tomlinson
Paul Severing
Percy Brebner
Peter B. Kyne
Plato
R. Derby Holmes
R. L. Stevenson
R. S. Ball
Rabindranath Tagore
Rahul Alvares
Ralph Bonehill
Ralph Henry Barbour
Ralph Victor
Ralph Waldo Emmerson
Rene Descartes
Rex Beach

Rex E. Beach
Richard Harding Davis
Richard Jefferies
Richard Le Gallienne
Robert Barr
Robert Frost
Robert Gordon Anderson
Robert L. Drake
Robert Lansing
Robert Lynd
Robert Michael Ballantyne
Robert W. Chambers
Rosa Nouchette Carey
Rudyard Kipling
Samuel B. Allison
Samuel Hopkins Adams
Sarah Bernhardt
Sarah C. Hallowell
Selma Lagerlof
Sherwood Anderson
Sigmund Freud
Standish O'Grady
Stanley Weyman
Stella Benson
Stella M. Francis
Stephen Crane
Stewart Edward White
Stijn Streuvels
Swami Abhedananda
Swami Parmananda
T. S. Ackland
T. S. Arthur
The Princess Der Ling
Thomas A. Janvier
Thomas A Kempis
Thomas Anderton
Thomas Bailey Aldrich
Thomas Bulfinch
Thomas De Quincey
Thomas Dixon

Thomas H. Huxley
Thomas Hardy
Thomas More
Thornton W. Burgess
U. S. Grant
Valentine Williams
Various Authors
Vaughan Kester
Victor Appleton
Victoria Cross
Virginia Woolf
Wadsworth Camp
Walter Camp
Walter Scott
Washington Irving
Wilbur Lawton
Wilkie Collins
Willa Cather
Willard F. Baker
William Dean Howells
William le Queux
W. Makepeace Thackeray
William W. Walter
William Shakespeare
Winston Churchill
Yei Theodora Ozaki
Yogi Ramacharaka
Young E. Allison
Zane Grey

www.ingramcontent.com/pod-product-compliance
Lightning Source LLC
Chambersburg PA
CBHW020500100426
42813CB00030B/3051/J